REPORTING FACTS AND RUNNING FROM THE TRUTH

A TV Anchor's Struggle to Find Self-Worth beyond a Job Title

ERIN LOGAN

CONTRIBUTOR
DONALD L. LOGAN

PAGE PUBLISHING, INC.
Conneaut Lake, PA

First originally published by Page Publishing 2021

ISBN 978-1-6624-4576-7 (pbk)
ISBN 978-1-6624-4577-4 (digital)

Printed in the United States of America

CONTENTS

Acknowledgments

To my parents, Tina and Don Logan; my grandparents, Norma and George Antonioni; and my best friends since college, Dr. Deb Prinz-Gentile and Jennifer DeStefano Stagnitti—thank you for the unconditional love and support throughout this journey. I could never have made it without you.

To all of my Connecticut friends—Lisa, Nancy, Solange, Jamie, Charlie, Tony, and many former coworkers there—thank you. You've all inspired me to get this book started. From 2011 to 2018, I called Connecticut home, and you all made me feel welcome.

Wendy Perrotti, my life coach and now friend, thank you for holding me accountable and believing in me. Also, thank you for your contribution in one of the chapters.

Gary Brown, Steve Doerr, Jon Hitchcock, John Bell, and BJ Finnell, thank you for making me feel like a valuable employee and for always encouraging me to hold my head high. Also, thank you, Steve, for your contribution in one of the chapters.

Jeremy Thurber, a longtime friend, thank you for your patience while helping me get all of these pages and photos organized.

Me and my Dad   Me and Jeremy Thurber

INTRODUCTION

It's May 2020 in the middle of the COVID-19 pandemic. At this point, the phrase "If you can't finish a project during this time, you never will" has become very clear. Shortly after this horrible, unfortunate mug shot on the cover of this book happened in 2010, there was never a question of whether I would write a book. The book's title, *Reporting Facts and Running from the Truth*, was decided almost immediately. My job as a news anchor and reporter has always been to "report facts." As far back as senior year in high school, I was "running from the truth." I figured by 2015, I would be ready to write, but that would've been the worst time. I was thirty-seven and fearing that the BIG four-zero was creeping up on me. I was engaged, then not engaged, and switching jobs from one station to another in Connecticut.

In elementary school, I said I wanted to go to a good college, be on the news, be in shape, and the list went on. I went to two unbelievable colleges, and I've been on the air in four top-twenty news markets—New York, Boston, Orlando, and Cleveland. However, I never really gave myself any credit for accomplishing these goals. I still thought I was a failure. You can only imagine how difficult it was (still is at times) for my parents to see me tormenting myself and never really looking at the real picture. I was never living in the present, was focused on the past as the fat kid who never made sports teams when all my friends did, always panicked about people judging me from one ridiculous night in South Bend, and was fearful of the future and failing. My hope is that you, your friends, or your children will learn from some of the mistakes I've made and the valuable lessons I've learned. I'm still learning.

The book may shift from different periods of time in my life in certain chapters. There will be some quotes from people who helped me, motivated me, and challenged me throughout this journey. At the end of this introduction and some of the chapters, you will hear from my dad, Don Logan. I wish I could go back to my old email accounts and share some of the emails he's sent me from 2008 until now. For TWELVE years, he's been sending every motivational quote, story, and words of advice to keep me from doing what he says is "taking a hammer and hitting yourself over your head" and from repeating some of the same mistakes.

To give you some perspective, he grew up in a very different scenario than I did. He was the oldest of many half-siblings, and his mother really struggled daily to make ends meet and put food on the table. Everything he accomplished, he did on his own. I grew up with two loving parents, grandparents, and was an only child until I was almost seven. My brother and I were spoiled with attention. If we were having a bad day, felt down, needed help with homework or some extra cash to go to a movie, we were never denied. My parents refinanced their home for me to go to Syracuse University and Boston University for graduate school. You can only imagine how annoying, stressful, and dumbfounded my dad was when I would complain about how awful my circumstances were as he was spending half his day for years on end trying to show me the "truth" that I am okay. I am lucky. All I kept doing was ignoring the "truth" and just kept using my job, "reporting the facts," as a distraction. At the end of the day, all that did was lead to loneliness and lack of fixing the real problem at hand: learning to like myself. If you don't like yourself, you're in for a rough road ahead.

Dad's Thoughts on My Desire to Write This Book

Monday, June 1, 2020

Wow. What can I say? You're finally on the path to revealing (to yourself) who you are and how you got there. Having lived the drama, I'm confident the readers, vicariously, will feel the searing highs and lows, the triumphs and defeats. I sense the writing will be a cathartic event. Not sure how it will end, but personally, I am a sucker for happy endings. The tone and tenor of the introduction give me much hope.

CHAPTER 1

YOU'RE YOUR OWN WORST ENEMY

On Thursday, April 15, 2010, I basically blew up my own world and all of the hard work I put in for eight years in the news business. Having a few drinks while depressed and then calling the cops for attention is not a good idea. I'll get to that situation shortly.

I started working in South Bend, Indiana, in April 2007. I was days away from completing a three-year contract as the 5:30 p.m. anchor. I would've been able to walk away with a good recommendation had the drunken arrest that I brought upon myself not happened. Anyone in the news business, or really any business, knows how small it is and how important it is to leave on good terms and complete a contract. I was told months in advance that my position was being eliminated. The station already had two longtime legend anchors, and there wasn't a need for a third anchor to do just a half-hour show. They weren't lying. To this day, more than ten years later, the station never brought back that position. I knew I wanted to move on to a new market when my contract was over, yet some part of me at that time thought I was being lied to and they didn't think I was good enough.

I had an agent, and we had a few months to find me a new gig before my contract was up. As it got closer, we weren't finding anything that clicked with my career goals at that point in time. I had already reported in Boston and Orlando. The gig in South Bend was a big step back in market size, but I took the job to get some main anchor experience and to have my weekends free. I started to panic as the sixty-day mark was approaching. Still no job offers that made sense to entertain. Then, the thirty-day mark. Still nothing. I got so nervous, scared, confused, and embarrassed. Was my career over? Was I just bad on air?

I was never a fan of the saying, "Timing is everything." The older I get, the more I realize it's so true. In the news business, it's not uncommon to have to wait a month or two in between jobs if you can't find one that lines up exactly after your previous contract comes to an end. Instead of being patient and knowing that something would come along that made sense, I started to self-destruct.

During some of my time in South Bend, I dated a former NFL football player and Notre Dame alum, who was on the 1988 championship football team and even inducted into the College Football Hall of Fame. We often talked about how much pressure we put on ourselves professionally. He had gone back to Notre Dame to get a law degree after playing several years in the NFL. I thought that was very impressive. I had also done some reporting in Boston and Orlando while in my twenties. I had teaching experience at the collegiate level, and I was known as a really hard worker who was determined to keep doing well. However, we often commiserated how we were so far from having our dream jobs. I think deep down we both knew that we would find much better positions somewhere given past accomplishments. It sounds easy to just "believe" that better days were ahead. For me, it was unbearable. I would call my dad, crying every single day, saying, "I would rather die than have people know I'm leaving here without a job."

I felt like everything around me was falling apart. It was mid-April, and I had no idea at all where I was going or what I was doing. The idea of moving back to my parents' home in Massachusetts and sleeping in my childhood bedroom at thirty-one years old seemed like a nightmare. I absolutely love spending time with my parents, but this seemed like too much.

As I mentioned, I was days away from successfully completing that three-year contract. It was less than three weeks to be exact. I was so incredibly depressed. The thought of leaving the area with no job to go to and having unresolved issues with a guy that I cared about at that time was too much. I thought I was the biggest failure ever to walk the face of the earth. Well, after that "call for help" to the police for no reason, I certainly turned out to publicly look like a hot mess failure.

I remember the start of this nightmare Thursday perfectly. I had the day off because I had some vacation time to burn. I was on my way to Chicago just for the day to do a high-paid freelance gig for a job advertising show. Basically, you show up looking pretty, read the teleprompter, and go on your way. I had my hair and makeup done and was wearing a beautiful red suit with very high platform heels. On the way back from Chicago, I decided to go to a restaurant bar close to where I lived. I remember the one drink I had. It was a martini with EFFEN black cherry vodka. I felt a little tipsy because I hadn't eaten much. I decided to text the guy and ask if we could speak. He said to go to his house.

I remember having a decent conversation and then a few too many drinks for my size. I was crying, upset, and feeling like a failure all over again after I just had a decent afternoon in Chicago. Instead of calling a friend for a ride, something came over me. I wanted to either get run over or die. Bottom line, I just wanted to get the hell out of South Bend. I couldn't take it anymore. The ship had sailed in that relationship. He was incredibly nice to me in the beginning. But it had been over for a while, and I clearly wasn't ready to walk away.

In that moment, I can't really tell you what I was thinking. I wasn't. I was drinking and was an emotional wreck. I called the non-emergency police line. He then called 911. Why wouldn't he? I had just called for no reason when I was the one acting like an idiot.

A female officer showed up and asked us to step outside. She offered to drive me home. I was clearly in no condition to drive, nor did I make any attempt. I got in the cruiser. She never really spoke to me, and I got agitated and told her to call one of the higher-ups. (On a side note, this police department, Mishawaka, used me as a guest speaker in classrooms. I was considered a role model. Wow. Anything but on this night.) The officer then told me to get back in the car, and she would drive me home as she previously stated. I kept talking and crying, and she said she would arrest me for disorderly conduct if I didn't stop. I still didn't listen. So she asked me to take the Breathalyzer. Now, I'm terrified, so I complied because I didn't know what else to do. I blew a .11 which is over the .08 legal limit. Apparently, I kept telling her to call higher-ups; so she arrested me for disorderly conduct, public intoxication, and resisting arrest. I spent the night in the county jail in the beautiful red pantsuit. I was welcomed by an older man who worked there. He was brought to tears as he saw the "news lady" in handcuffs. Looking at the camera to take that mug shot took forever. I couldn't look straight ahead. Fast forward, the charges were never filed, and I never stepped foot in court. But man, oh man, did I suffer the consequences.

I was able to make one phone call that night. I don't know why, but I called my parents in the early morning hours. My mom was really upset. My dad said, "I'm not surprised. I told you to hang in there, complete the remaining days of your contract, stay away from people that you know are going to upset you, and leave on a positive note." I did the polar opposite and went out with a bang. I ended up spending eight hours in a cell by myself. I cried and cried and cried. After what seemed like an eternity, they told me I could leave. I posted the $250 bail and called my friend, Mindy, for a ride. She gave me a hug and cried. She already saw the mug shot a dozen times. It was plastered in the newspapers, and the arrest was mentioned on all of the local news stations. When you're in the public eye and you get arrested, it certainly doesn't take long for people to find out.

I immediately called my friend, Lenny Zappia, who was (still is) an attorney in town. He prepared me for what may or may not happen. He did say, "The one thing you have going for you is people in the community see you as a news anchor, college instructor, and volunteer for charitable events, but I'm warning you. The police report is very colorful." He wasn't lying. I wanted to throw up over the line from some tabloid website: "The officer had to forcibly lift Logan out of the car. In the process, Logan lifted her three-inch heels [they were higher than that!] aggressively and put her hands up and tried to swat at the officer." To this day ten years later, some idiots still say, "Dude, you kicked the cop." Really? I'm pretty sure I would've been arrested or charged with trying to assault a police officer if that were the case.

Not even an hour after hanging up with Lenny, I got a phone call from my bosses who fired me effective immediately. I got FIRED even though I only had DAYS left on my contract. Of course, that was never mentioned anywhere. Some companies have a zero tolerance policy in the contract that states if you do anything to put the company in a negative light, you're fired. So in this case, it's guilty until proven innocent. I know TV news people who were arrested for child pornography who were not FIRED until the courts decided their fate. Again, different company, different policy. So as I mentioned, I went out with a bang—A BIG BANG!

The following days were tough. They were awful. The talk on the internet, the gossip, the rumors—it was all too much to handle. I remember going to Walmart and some lady was staring at me, saying, "Are you that news lady?" She talked to me as if I were a murder suspect. It was beyond humiliating. That mug shot was everywhere! Some TV station websites wrote their articles as if I just showed up at some random guy's house drunk. Then, a group of Notre Dame students, who were in a band, wrote a full-blown song about me called "The Ballad of Erin Logan." I will say it is quite catchy; and the lyrics are very interesting, referring to my night spent in jail and some of the other anchors that were on the same newscast. My younger brother's friends got a kick out of it. At the time, I cried and cringed every time someone brought it up. Now, I crack up because it's ridiculous people would put that much time and effort into something so stupid.

One would assume that since I got fired and was publicly humiliated, that I would want to get the heck out of South Bend even more than I did before the arrest. Wrong. I was determined to stick around and clear my name. I went back and forth with my attorney. I had to write and rewrite apology letters so many times to the police. At the end of the day, that's what happened. I mouthed off to a female officer. I was drunk, and I was emotional. I called the cops and ran my mouth at the responding female officer for no reason other than, I'm guessing, attention at the time.

Roughly six weeks later, the prosecutor decided not to file charges after speaking at length to the arresting officer and the chief. Other members of the police department also knew me personally. As I mentioned, I worked closely with officers while covering stories and as a classroom speaker for the DARE program, which stands for "Drug Abuse Resistance Education." Lieutenant Tim Williams of the Mishawaka, Indiana Police Department recently provided this statement when I told him about my reasons for writing this book.

> I had the pleasure of getting to know Erin while she was working locally as an Anchor. I found Erin to be a strong, confident professional woman. I asked Erin to be a role model for my D.A.R.E. Program knowing that she would inspire young girls to follow their dreams. Near the end of Erin's contract at the station, I watched this strong, confident woman become unsure of herself doubting who she was and what she was going to do. This change was devastating to see. Whenever I had the chance, I would encourage Erin to believe in herself and the woman she is, a strong confident woman. The night she got into trouble certainly seemed out of character. (June 2020)

During the "wait and see" period before the prosecutor made a decision, I spent about two weeks living in the Cleveland area at one of my best friends' (Deb) and college roommates' childhood home. I stayed with her mom Nina who I loved dearly. She has since passed. How weird is that? Fast forward all these years later and here I am working in Cleveland, which is what Nina had always hoped for. Anyway, I wanted to stay close enough to South Bend until I knew that the charges were dropped. I think I would've gone out of my mind if I went back to Massachusetts (fourteen hours from South Bend) and waited at my parents' house. Not to mention, Nina had some sort of way with her that made everyone feel so at ease.

During my stay at Nina's, I couldn't help but google myself fifty times a day to see what other crap was being said about me. I got a lot of phone calls from previous bosses who were willing to help and others who I knew really liked me and respected my work but said, "Logan, I'm not sure if you will recover from this because there are so many others out there who are just as good as you, but don't have a mug shot." I didn't let that comment discourage me. If anything, it made me even more determined to get back out there and show everyone I had a good résumé, good work ethic, and good character—minus one bad night.

I got the call I had been waiting for from Gary Brown, a former boss in Providence. I had freelanced for him in 2004. You will hear A LOT about him in chapter 4 (The Broadcast Journey). He was long gone from Providence, but he knew that there was a reporter opening at one of the other stations there and that Providence was just forty-five minutes from my family, which was where I needed to be after going through all of that humiliation. It was a step backward professionally (anchor to reporter), but it would get me back on the air in an area that I knew so well and loved. He put me in touch with the general manager, Steve Doerr, and the news director, BJ Finnell. I'm forever grateful to all of them. They believed in me and made me feel welcome.

Again, the arrest was April 15, 2010. The charges were dropped in early June. By mid-June, I accepted the job in Providence and was on the air by the end of June 2010. It was the most nerve-wracking time of my life. I blew up my whole world and had to build it all back up. Sadly, up until 2019, I felt like I was still playing catch-up. This experience affected me in so many ways. It made me turn to work even more to mask my feelings. I continued to "report facts" and "run from the truth." For the next four years, all I cared about was gaining back my credibility. I put my social life on hold and never really addressed the pain and trauma of what really led me to hit rock bottom. The experience made me a fighter but also made me afraid of trusting people and fully believing in myself.

We'll pick up on this time period in chapter 4, which discusses my career path. Since this book addresses specific topics and lessons learned, I want to start with my childhood and how being overweight really had an effect on my life and my self-esteem. First though…

Dad's Comments

The unexamined life is not worth living. (Socrates)

Having read the introduction and chapter 1, it appears that Erin thinks I have some sage understandings to impart. Not really. It's just that I'm twenty-eight years her senior and have, from experience, seen and felt some of what she has felt and is expressing. Our paths to adulthood are different but similar in that we have both self-destructed, felt the shame of it, and continued to stand tall and work through it. It seems a bitter lesson is one earned but worth remembering. I have many since I was what one would call a knucklehead. After six years and four colleges, I had gathered a total of two years' credits. I did gain a lot of "worldly knowledge" in the painstaking process. Fortunately, a great wife, two kids, and supporting family and friends have done much to scrape the knuckles off my knuckleheadedness. It's still there but doesn't pop up every other minute. Just so you know.

Much of the background and many of the details Erin has revealed, so far, are new to me. Her candidness is shocking but courageous at the same time. What is clear is that she truly wanted to take a hard, unvarnished look at herself and her actions and help others in the process; to examine the whys and wherefores; and to arrive at a better, peaceful place in her mind. The fact that in the introduction she mentioned "learning to like yourself" gives me hope that she is indeed running to the truth. One has to have compassion for oneself in order to not self-destruct. The mind is our constant companion. We have to make peace with it, control it, or it will crush you. We can cope, just barely, with distractions, but they are temporary. A quiet mind is our best companion. It does not make reality appear better than what it is or worse. That is the province of the loud mind, a.k.a. the monkey mind. Regrettably, from my observations, Erin would routinely succumb to resurrecting or recreating the past or wildly projecting what the future will hold. From some of her off-the-cuff reflections, her mind director at times was deserving of an Oscar. Imaginative, to say the least. Sadly, one cannot have clear thinking while listening to the cacophony of relentless monkey chatter in the back of our heads. Without clear thinking, we make poor decisions. Poor decisions inevitably spawn poor results. This leads to unhappiness and further mind projections of the future. This unfortunate cycle goes on and on.

Chapter 1: "You're Your Own Worst Enemy" is replete with these mind projections which haunted her thinking and thus her decisions. Some examples are "Was I bad on air?" "I would rather die than have people know I'm leaving without a job," "The biggest failure to walk the earth," "The talk on the internet, the gossip, the rumors," and "Yes, it was all too much to handle." With all the foregoing in her mind and not being able to process it, no wonder she lost it.

"Timing is everything." Erin was never a fan of the saying. It's likely because if I used it once with her, I'm sure I said it twenty times. You see, Erin struggled to look at situations in a nuanced way in the past. It was all an equation for her. If you worked extremely hard, you should be rewarded. When that didn't happen, the equation was, "I'm not good enough, not pretty enough, not smart enough." This of course put her creative mind in a warp mode.

I'll end with this. Given her breathtaking openness and frankness about her own actions, it's clear she's beginning to laugh at her demons and their silliness.

CHAPTER 2

CHUBBY CHILDHOOD TRAUMA

Five generations

I don't know if it's possible to have had a better childhood as far as love, attention, and role models surrounding me. Not only do I have two loving parents but grandparents (my mom's parents) who are still alive in 2020 at ninety-two and ninety-three years old. Incredible. It gets better. I even had the chance to meet TWO of my great-grandmothers and a great-great-grandmother. I included a picture showing five generations! In fact, one of my great-grandmothers was alive until I was nineteen, so I got to spend a lot of time with her. Talk about being blessed!

My cousin David and I were the youngest of a big group of cousins and were showered with love and attention. We had more fun at Sunday dinners at Nonna's house, holidays, and birthday celebrations every year for every single family member. That right there counts for a lot of family time.

My grandfather was the principal at the high school in my hometown, and my mother was a kindergarten and third-grade teacher for more than forty years. Everyone knew my family by having one or both of them in school. My cousin Bobby was a state representative and state senator for many years, so he too is well-known. I think you get the picture that I come from a tight-knit family that valued education.

Every therapist I've ever spoken with has said, "You must have had some type of childhood trauma contributing to this low self-esteem. Did your parents belittle you?" The answer is "HELL NO, my parents never made me feel bad about myself...ever!" For the first six and a half years of my life, I was an only child. My parents were kind and loving. I have amazing memories of the camping trips my dad would plan for us, his buddies, and their daughters. I feel like up until ten years old, I was the happiest kid without a care in the world. My dad, nicknamed "CHOPPER," even coached the basketball teams I was on to show support. He never once thought, *I'm embarrassed that my kid can't run. She's huffing and puffing and already has little boobs bouncing around at ten years old.* He was the MOST FIT, ATHLETIC DAD with the CHUBBIEST MOST AWKWARD DAUGHTER running the court. At the end of the day, he couldn't have cared less. I was his daughter, and he was proud.

As all parents know, even before social media, kids were mean. I can't even imagine what you're forced to deal with when your child gets picked on publicly today. I would say at around age ten, I started to have some self-doubt. As I just described, I was chubby. I always, always had friends around me because I was super friendly. I was never the girl that guys thought was cute, but they definitely would laugh and joke with me. I was a straight-A student, so that was kind of cool to be noticed at least for that. That seemed to be my "fire back" ammunition when kids started calling me "fatty." I would say, "Whatever, dummy." Two wrongs don't make a right, but back then, all parents told kids to stand up for themselves and say something back.

Let's fast-forward to junior high school. I REALLY got big. It was at this time that the doctors realized I had hypothyroidism, which is an inactive thyroid. I started abruptly gaining more weight. I weighed 170 pounds at twelve years old. I think I was five foot three at the time. That's not healthy. My mom took me to the doctor, and he did some blood work. And that's when I was diagnosed. I still didn't really take it upon myself to go on a strict diet, and my parents never made comments encouraging me to lose weight. I'm guessing they didn't want to make me feel bad. I don't know. Dad will chime in about that shortly. I still went about my business; played sports being overweight; and hung out with the popular, pretty people because of my fun personality. I was picked on here and there; but there was a defining moment that made me say to myself, "I need to lose weight. I'm tired of being the ugly duckling in the group."

Eighth grade dance with Katie Hudson

I will never forget the eighth-grade end-of-the-year dance. Parents were invited to come in at the end and mingle. All night long, not one person asked me to dance. I was so embarrassed and felt like I wanted to crawl in a cave. I remember clear as day looking at my mom and saying, "I'm tired of being rejected from everything and everyone because I'm fat."

My mom hugged me and said, "You have a beautiful face, and I will help you lose some weight. You can do this."

When we got in the car, I gave more specifics about my rejection comment. Once hitting a certain age, there were sports you had to try out for and make the team. All my friends, every single last one of them, would make the cheerleading team. Not fat Erin. I was always on the "reject team," meaning you can still be on a team but with the younger girls. I remember being devastated for not making those teams two years in a row, but it wasn't until THIS moment at that dance that I just couldn't take it anymore. My heart was broken because I felt so worthless. Boys didn't like me, and coaches didn't want me on their team. In my hometown, cheering for Pop Warner football was the biggest thing. If you weren't on the teams in your age range, it was beyond embarrassing. This may sound so miniscule to some people. I had the kick-ass family who loved and supported me, so who cares about petty things? Well, it was the following years and years of self-doubt that made being the fat horrible athlete as a child so traumatizing into adult life. Hence, "Chubby Childhood Trauma."

In high school, things started out the same. I gave sports a shot, but I just ended up feeling embarrassed as I was not very good. My friends were terrific and walked away from every sporting event feeling great. For some reason, I still stuck with it during freshman year. Then, I decided to try something new and get involved in theater arts. I remember my friends laughing at me, but I didn't care. I definitely was not a follower. I wore what I wanted and started to have friends from all different walks of life. Some were good news; some were bad news. The bottom line is I had a lot of friends and people who wanted me around. I was a star student; but I wasn't the pretty, most popular girl who people simply adored. After several years of taking a backseat to everyone, I decided to stop TALKING about losing weight and being more athletic and start DOING it.

It all happened in junior year. My cousin, John, played a big role in firing me up to live a fit, healthy lifestyle. He was twenty-five at the time, and I was sixteen when I approached him about going to the gym. There was a popular gym in town called Orchard Hills, but you had to be eighteen to be a member. I asked him if he would put me on his membership, and he said yes without hesitation. Before I go any further, I said we "were" close because John is no longer with us. He took his own life at the age of twenty-nine. This was truly devastating as he had the looks, the charm, the intelligence, and a wonderful family.

I started out going to some aerobics classes, running a little on the treadmill, and eating healthier. Ironically, this mid-1990s era was all about ZERO FAT and ALL CARBS! Wow, times have changed when it comes to dieting (more on that in a later chapter). I saw gradual results, and it kept motivating me more and more. It started to become a commitment. While my friends were at their softball practice or basketball, I would be at the gym. By winter, I started to feel a little thinner, so I went back to cheerleading. At this point, I didn't feel like I got rejected to the bad team because a lot of the girls wanted to cheer for ice hockey instead of basketball. It was a lot of fun. I have great memories. I even went to a summer camp and didn't feel like the awkward fatty in the tight shorts running the field. I knew 138 pounds wasn't exactly where I needed to be, but it was a lot better than 170 or whatever it was a few years back!

Senior year, I was still losing weight and feeling great. I was not in the 120s, where I probably should've been, but I started to feel better for many other reasons. I got accepted early decision to Syracuse University. I was Homecoming Queen, followed by Miss Massachusetts Homecoming Queen. I won most popular and best dressed, and things were starting to go as I had always hoped. The excitement lasted for a few months. At the end of the day though, it set the stage for me, taking it to a whole other level as far as being an overachiever. The thought process was *I'm still not thin enough. I'm still not pretty enough. I'm still not smart enough.* This was all reflected in many of my choices in boys I liked in high school. One of them always had a girlfriend, yet I was always around when he would break up with them. I was always second choice for everything else and figured why would that be anything different. It's interesting though that even when hanging out with a guy (three years older) and his friends who were all into heavy drugs, I never did do or try them when asked multiple times. Even with all of my insecurities, I still felt secure in my intelligence and standing my ground with not being peer pressured. Did I do marijuana a little bit? Sure. I never tried one other drug though, and there were tons around.

I would be lying if I said I didn't do my fair share of partying in high school as far as drinking. All the girls I hung out with came from good families, so none of this was a result of bad parenting. We were all straight-A students just wanting to have fun a year or two earlier than the start of college. One of the girls had an older brother. One had an older sister, so we were able to stay at their houses and have drinks when the parents went to bed on the other side of the home. At my house, that was a whole different story. I was the oldest. If I was seventeen, my brother was ten or eleven. I remember he found empty bottles in my closet and gave them to my parents. Also, my parents' room is upstairs, so we all stupidly thought they wouldn't hear us sneaking people in and out of my window! I had this little bench outside the window that people would use as a stool to get in and out! That didn't last long. I got in big trouble. When I got yelled at, I would slam the door, which led my dad to take the door off the hinges! That meant at seventeen, I had no bedroom door for a while, had no privacy, had to whisper on the phone, and the list goes on. I believe it's safe to say that I drove my parents nuts my senior year. However, doing some high school partying DEFINETLY helped as I transitioned to life on my own five hours away at Syracuse University. College days are up next. But first...

Dad's Comments

I have to say that in reading "Chubby Childhood Trauma," there were many instances that were brought up that I was completely unaware of. Granted, I wasn't aware of your internal self-doubts and the slights you felt, but I was also clueless about the extent of underage drinking. Shocking. At the time, your mother and I thought we were doing our best to stem the partying. If you were having friends over, we tried to respect your space, yet keep a watchful eye, and not be overly intrusive while giving our best due diligence. When I learned that friends (uninvited guests) were sneaking into a window on the adjacent porch, I installed a motion sensor light which fully lit up the area. I gleefully conjured up mental images of the first few entrants when they got illuminated. When you got annoyed with your little brother walking into your friend-filled bedroom and slamming the door numerous times, I removed it. I did say that when you apologized for almost breaking the door, I would return it. Your stubbornness and attitude wouldn't allow you to. I finally put it back on when you went away to college. We assumed that when at your friend's houses that their parents were similarly being watchful. Given your good grades and that of your friends, the many sports and school activities that you were all involved in, we felt confident that your common sense and decency would not lead you down the wrong path.

The "chubbiness" perception you later felt was never an issue with your mother and me. Indeed, as a baby, you were not chubby. As an elementary school teacher, your mother had eight weeks' maternity leave, and then went back to full-time teaching. Breastfeeding was not an option. We therefore used the baby formula recommended by your pediatrician. Your newly forming gastrointestinal system didn't approve of the formula nor any and all of the replacements which were done one after the other. As a last resort, the pediatrician threw up his hands and said all he could think of was a meat-based formula. It looked and smelled like a dog food gruel. Incredibly, your digestive system took to it, and you started to thrive. When you were able to start eating more solid food, you leaned toward ground-up hamburger and meats. When we started taking you out to dinner with us, we always circled back to Mickey D's or Burger King since you had little or no interest in what we were having. By the age of three and four, you were pleasingly chubby but also a happy child. When you started elementary school, you had a solid frame, not slight. Since I was six feet, four inches and 250 pounds, I assumed your build was a reflection of me. You were bright, energetic, always smiling, and very talkative (you are your mother's daughter too). There was nothing to be alarmed about. You would grow out of the chubby phase. We focused on your education and socialization skills. End of story.

By the time you got to junior high school, your mother and I began to sense some unease on your part with your physique. There again, we didn't make an issue of it. Your mom found a number of photos of herself at the same age. She too was a little chubby but cute. We were confident you would grow out of the weight issue. Heaven knows you were active enough, always moving, always up to something.

By mid-high school, we knew you were very conscious of your weight. I was advised of it through your mother since it was not something you, nor I, talked about. Thank heavens for her empathy and support as she took the full brunt of your unhappiness. I recall many tear-filled nights that she listened to and absorbed your frustrations. Personally, I think she felt your pain as much as or more. It bothered her tremendously. I simply focused on better meal selection and keeping you busy.

I do remember your suddenly taking a keen interest in working out. Simultaneously, you became a calorie counter and food fanatic. God forbid we put a tab of butter on the salmon fillet or used a ranch dressing on a salad. Orange juice, high in fructose sugar, was a no-no. Your mom and I just went with the flow. Another adolescent stage to contend with. Let's just try to get through it.

In short order, you were active and happy in doing theater. You seemed to thrive being on stage. Next was being selected Homecoming Queen. Not because of Helen of Troy beauty but because you got along with and treated everyone as a friend. Massachusetts Homecoming Queen led to the nationals at Disney Land.

I'll end with this. One of my best childhood friends has two beautiful accomplished daughters. He wouldn't offer a compliment to anyone even if he was paid to do so. I know because he has never given me a single compliment. That's just who he is. He is a hard man. In any event, he took me aside one day and told me he has never seen anyone completely transform their body and do it naturally by the force of their sheer will. He said no one, bar none. I couldn't agree more. I'm the reasonable one. I'm saddened the self-doubt continued even with this healthy lifestyle you were committed to and saw results with and the early acceptance to Syracuse University. These were your accomplishments you worked at and succeeded.

Me as a happy
five-year-old

Grandparents, Norma
and George

Me and my
brother, Ryan

Mom and Dad

CHAPTER 3

IN THE GAME BUT STILL FEELING BENCHED

August 1996, I can't believe that was twenty-four years ago. Unreal. My parents dropped me off at Syracuse University and helped me unpack and set up my dorm at Day Hall. When the moment came for them to say their goodbyes and leave, it was awkward, and I felt like I had a pit in my stomach. My mother looked at me as I started to cry and said, "You don't have to stay if you don't want." You could see the look in my dad's eyes as he wanted to say to her, "What the hell are you doing? She hasn't even spent an hour here on her own." They ended up leaving a few minutes after, and I was just fine. I was lucky to have met my roommate over the summer and hang out a few times. Looking back, this is all funny to me because here was the girl who was dying to be on her own with no rules, yet I was terrified.

The first semester was one to remember. How I managed to go to the gym, go to every single one of my classes, go out five nights a week, yet still get a 3.9 GPA is insane. However, I was a nervous wreck all the time, constantly doubting myself and my ability to do well in class. I think, or I actually know, that it's because I often had my parents check my homework. I feel very fortunate for that, believe me. I was just afraid that I would be "not so successful" if I didn't have those second set of eyes. It's kind of ridiculous I thought that way because they weren't there in class taking my tests with me hundreds of times before college. I did just fine. I was always a high-honors student, sometimes even straight As—minus math of course.

I was very mature when it came to my main priority: being successful in the classroom. I wanted to make my parents proud because I knew how much money they were spending for me to go there. In fact, they refinanced their home to make that possible. For that, I am forever grateful. I'm also glad I had a relationship with them where they knew I was a typical college teen who would go to parties occasionally. They didn't have their blinders on like some of the other kids' parents I met the first year of college. Those kids were the ones who partied like rock stars, blew off class, and failed out pretty quickly.

Second semester of freshman year was a big one. Syracuse University is known for its huge number of fraternities and sororities. Everyone in the dorm was talking about rush and knowing which house they wanted to be in as they were familiar with "cool" ones from older siblings or friends. I remember feeling like a complete idiot and waaaaay out of place. Most of these girls were dressed to the nines, hair and makeup impeccable, and seemed so self-assured. You could tell most of their families were loaded with money and paid out of pocket in full for their tuition. These girls asked what my parents did for a living; and I said with pride, "My mom is a teacher, and my dad sells insurance." I didn't lie like some others and say my parents owned an empire.

I remember walking in all the dozen-plus sorority homes with my short black hair, an eyebrow ring, a lot of jewelry, and outfits that were a little different. I will say this a hundred times. I always wore what I wanted and didn't care what people thought. It seems odd coming from someone with really bad body-image issues at that time. I think my ability to be REAL and connect with all types of people was and still is my most attractive attribute. Anyway, whatever or however I showed up seemed to have worked. I got asked back to all the houses that I liked. This was after I called my parents the night before saying that I don't think the three houses I really liked were interested. I guess I was wrong. I was "in the game," but based on childhood experiences, I still felt "benched."

After the whole process was over, I ended up choosing Delta Gamma, and they chose me. The funny part is that the president of the Greek association just so happened to be in that home. I met her during the whole rush process, and she clearly wasn't allowed to let on which house she was in. All she said on the final night was "I hope you end up in the home that you really want." Sure enough, I ended up in her home. Here we are twenty-four years later, still best friends, and ironically, we live three miles away. Who would've thought I would end up getting an anchor job in Deb Prinz's hometown of Cleveland? It's so sad because her mom Nina, who I mentioned helped me through the South Bend incident, always wanted this to happen, yet she passed away in 2015.

Being in a sorority was something I never thought of doing before arriving at Syracuse. I'm so glad I did for a number of reasons. Most importantly, I met my best friends. Deb Prinz and Jenn DeStefano are still my best friends. I was the maid of honor in both of their weddings. I don't have a sister, so these two are like my big sisters. The sorority experience also helped me to be very disciplined. I lived in a house with twenty-plus girls. There was always a party to go to, food, drinks, drugs, etc. I never once tried any drug other than marijuana. I actually hated it. I didn't pig out and gain a ton of weight. I certainly wasn't thin in college, but I didn't blow up. There was always coercion to skip class, yet I RARELY skipped.

I really do have fond memories of Syracuse, especially when it comes to my major, which was speech communication. I always did excellent in all my courses because I truly enjoyed them. However, most of the students who wanted to be a news reporter or anchor were in the broadcast major in Newhouse School of Communications. Rather than switch majors in my junior year, I decided to stay the course and do some internships at local news stations to get some experience in that field. Speech communications taught me incredible speaking and writing skills, but I quickly learned broadcasting was a whole different animal. I had no idea what I was in for when I got my first internship acceptance.

Spring 1998 was extremely memorable. I was in a lot of high-level classes, was trying to make the most of sorority life and went to the many weekly functions at night, AND did well in my very first TV news internship. I remember it like it was yesterday. I walked in to the then FOX affiliate in Syracuse that had a 10:00 p.m. newscast. I figured with my personality, eagerness to learn, and really good writing skills (or so I thought) that I would do great. Not so much. After a whole semester of interning from 3:00 p.m. to 11:00 p.m., in addition to a full day of classes and homework, I felt like a failure. I did awesome in all my classes but NOT my internship. It was as if I could've cared less about the straight As and was so laser focused on this "average" score I received from my intern adviser, Joe Zone. He was the evening anchor at the time alongside Amy Kellogg, who went on to be an international correspondent for FOX News Channel. I'm smiling as I write this because the first on-camera practicing that I ever did for TV news was with Amy. She was super helpful and encouraging to interns. You could tell she wanted people to succeed. As for the AVERAGE score from Joe, I remember clear as day calling my dad from the back porch of my sorority home sobbing. He talked me off a ledge and told me to focus on the positive, take a breath, gather my thoughts, and then pick up the phone and call Joe to ask for feedback. I was terrified, but I made the call. I spoke with Joe at length, and he explained I was not one of his typical interns. The majority were students in Newhouse, the broadcast school, as I mentioned. They would walk in knowing, at the very least, the lingo used every day in a newsroom. Let's say if they were in fifth grade of TV news, I was in preschool. Therefore, Joe had every reason to give me an average score. This was all new territory. He could tell I was very serious about learning the business, so he offered me a summer internship. My parents graciously supported me and let me stay for a few weeks over the summer just so I could do this internship.

As summer rolled around, I was so excited. My best friend, Jenn, was from Syracuse, so we had an absolute blast. We both did our internships and still managed to have a lot of fun at the apartment I sublet for six weeks. I will say we had the "work hard, play hard" lifestyle down to a science. I ended up doing great on the internship this second go-around. I didn't get a stellar review, but it was leaps and bounds better than "AVERAGE" from the previous semester. I learned a lot and was given some really cool assignments from Joe that included writing some of his stories for the newscast. Amy was also great about letting me tag along if she went out to cover a story. She showed me a lot; and I remember thinking, *I will definitely help interns someday because of how at ease she made me feel.* Believe me. I had some other internships down the road that weren't nearly as pleasant.

Senior year came so fast! The class of 2000! The plan was for me to get a master's degree in broadcast journalism. I knew with absolute certainty that I wanted to be a news reporter and eventually an anchor. I did HORRIBLE on the GRE. HORRIBLE. I'm talking failure. It made no sense, considering the grades I was pulling. I will say though. I have never been good at multiple-choice tests. Fortunately, the schools I applied to looked past the test scores and focused more on my grades and my internships. I got accepted to Syracuse with a FULL scholarship, but there was a BUT. It wasn't in the broadcast school. I didn't apply to that school. I was highly encouraged by my professors to apply to the speech communications master's program because my exceptional grades would likely mean a full scholarship. I don't even know why I applied knowing that I wanted and needed more training in broadcasting in order to get a job in that field. Two days prior to graduation, I found out I was accepted to Boston University's broadcast journalism master's program with a partial academic scholarship. Based on my undergraduate success, my parents agreed to pay the rest because I needed to focus on learning the ropes in broadcasting. I promised them that I would pick up the phone BEFORE graduation and let my Syracuse professors know that I would be attending Boston University. It wasn't until I was on stage during the graduation ceremony that I informed the two professors who shook my hand. That was not one of my proudest moments. I still shake my head about how rude and inconsiderate I was. I was too wrapped up in my friends, my boyfriend, and just having fun that last semester. Fortunately, a fellow classmate, Steve, who REALLY wanted the full Syracuse scholarship, ended up taking my spot.

Fall 2000 was the start of graduate school at Boston University. It was a group of eighteen students from all over the world. I was honored to have been chosen as part of such a select group.

However, I kind of set myself up for a year of over-the-top stress and anxiety. I was the only one not living anywhere near Boston. I thought driving from Providence to Boston every day would be manageable. Without traffic, we're talking a forty-five-minute ride. During the morning commute, tack on another forty minutes at least. Then, factor in parking, walking to class, spending a full day there, doing homework, and driving back home. A typical day was waking up at 5:30 a.m. and arriving home at 10:00 p.m. I just had to live with my boyfriend though, who was working in Providence. It became way too much to handle. I felt like a child pretending to be a mature adult. My boyfriend became my fiancé just two months into my graduate program. I remember my professor and two of my internship advisers saying, in different words, "If you're thinking of getting married at twenty-two years old AND wanting to be an on-air reporter, you better think again UNLESS your man is willing to follow you around in the beginning of your career." I never forgot that statement, and I feel there is a lot of truth to that statement. We were both very ambitious in fields that would require moving around and putting our careers first. My least favorite statement, "Timing is everything"—it was so true in this case. I will get into this more in the chapter about relationships, but I was so far away from being ready to be a wife at twenty-two. I felt scared, sad, and confused.

There was a lot of back-and-forth between us for months, so I ended up living at home and commuting to school. I slept on people's floors and ruined the whole graduate school experience. I got good grades, but I wasn't my rock star self like I was in the classroom at Syracuse. I couldn't separate my personal life from school. All I did was worry about, think about, and call the ex. There was no text or emailing from your cell phone back then, so it was like torture waiting for a return call. Through all of this chaos, I ended up winning an award with the girl I had partnered up with in the grad school program. It was for a story we put together that took nearly a whole semester. There was a ceremony for all the recipients and parents, and the awards were presented by prestigious members of the Boston media. When they called my name, I wasn't there, but my parents were. How embarrassing. I was too busy crying and arguing with the ex when I already knew it wasn't going to work out and my priority was school and pursuing an on-air job. That was also another "not one of my proudest" moments.

On paper, this program was three semesters. The last semester was basically to work on your creative project to be submitted. Instead, over the summer (after the first two semesters), I did a six-week on-air internship at the NBC affiliate in Missoula, Montana. Yes, Montana. When the offer was originally presented to the class, I didn't think I would apply because it was way too far away from home. I applied simply to see if I would be chosen. I was in fact chosen, and I made the scary yet rewarding decision to go for it. I got six credits for this experience and was able to put together a full-blown REAL résumé tape of stories that aired on live television. A lot of people starting out have tapes filled with on-camera work only from the classroom and not a real television station.

This experience set the stage for what was about to be one hell of a journey in the broadcast industry. Two of the girls, Dara and Alia, who worked there were my age. This was their first real job. They actually knew each other and were from California. We had a ball! They welcomed me, helped me out. We hung out, and all of us were so excited about covering the news. This was summer 2001. Ironically, I just heard from one of them days ago in 2020! You've got to love social media. Anyway, I will never forget a statement one of their mothers said to them regarding their fear of moving there from a big city. "This is not a death sentence. Make mistakes, learn, and build your résumé." It's so true. Some of the smaller places, like Missoula, are the most memorable—Moose Drool beer, fly fishing, intense hiking, drinking great coffee, and eating bags of delicious kettle corn late at night. What's wrong with that?

From September 2001 through November 2001, I must have dubbed one hundred VHS tapes to be boxed up and mailed at the post office. I spent a few bucks there. I ended up getting an offer at the CBS affiliate, the only local news station in Presque Isle, Maine, as the weekend anchor and weekday reporter. I thought, *Hey, Maine is close to Massachusetts where my family is.* UMM…wrong. It's seven hours north. But it was my first job, and I was excited.

Jennifer DeStefano-Stagnitti   Dr. Deb Prinz-Gentile

CHAPTER 4

THE BROADCAST JOURNEY FROM NORTH, SOUTH, WEST TO EAST AND BACK

Lights, camera, action. Some days, I don't know whether to call my life as a journalist an adventure, a joy, a nightmare, or a thrill. I will say this. On my worst day and as down in the dumps as I've been (and it's been low), there's something about the "lights" and being "live" that has helped put me at ease. I mean this for two reasons. When I'm on live television, I have no choice but to pull it together. I can't say when the clock strikes 5:00 p.m., "Oh, excuse me. Let me wipe my tears," or "Hold on. Let me read or send this text that I already know is going to make me feel worse." I have a snap second to pull it together. This picture I've included in the black jacket at the anchor desk was after bawling my eyes out over a very sad, personal situation. I still don't know how I managed to pull it together that day and many, many others. It's much easier to do this when you're at the anchor desk and there's a teleprompter. When you're reporting live in the field on breaking news in a complex court case and you're ad-libbing so many facts and names, it's a whole different program. It is mind-boggling that I was able to do this so many times after crying and not being in the right frame of mind. The other reason I'm saying the "lights" and being "live" have helped put me at ease is because this job is more than a job. It's a hobby. It's something that

I feel confident doing and that I earned on my own. No one ever once handed me a job. It's been tough, rewarding, and, on many occasions, has led to very low self-worth, but I have no regrets going after a profession I wanted since childhood. I'm blessed that I've had such supportive parents and grandparents to help me on this journey. Without their help in the beginning, I would've been starving. You will quickly notice my résumé looks like a hopscotch board. There were times when one would think, *Be done with this*. The timing just hasn't been right. When I know, I will know.

New Haven, Connecticut

Stop 1: Presque Isle, Maine—Market 205

If you don't know anything about television news markets, there are 210. The higher the number, the smaller the market. For example, New York, Los Angeles, Chicago, and Philadelphia are the top four. Presque Isle is 205, so I definitely started small. It was perfect though. They only made new talent sign a one-year contract. As I mentioned in the last chapter, I was hired as the weekend anchor/reporter. We only had Saturday shows on the weekend, so my days off were Sunday and Monday. I reported four days a week and went out in the field with a photographer. My job on Saturdays was to write and then anchor the entire shows for both the 6:00 p.m. and 11:00

p.m. Basically, I was my own producer. If a breaking news story had to be added or one needed to be dropped, I had the added pressure of trying to keep up with the show and make sure I was off air at let's say 6:28:15 p.m.! I don't remember any nightmare moments other than one. This one is hard to top. I didn't have enough time to print my scripts. You might think, *Well, no big deal, you have a teleprompter.* I learned the hard way just how unreliable a teleprompter was and still is. It can fail at any time, and it happens quite often. So here I am with no scripts and no teleprompter, which meant "What the hell story is next to read!" It's not like when you're reporting in the field and you have one specific story that you're familiar with. This was an entire newscast with many stories. I was so nervous. I remember tossing to commercial break. I truthfully don't remember what happened next. The experience was enough to make me realize how important it is to start small in this business or any business really. It's a lot better to make mistakes and learn from them in places where the audience is much smaller and aware that this is not the big time.

Most of the team was around my age, which made the experience really cool. We all helped one another out on the job, and we had a lot of fun on our off days. There wasn't exactly a huge nightlife in Presque Isle, but we made it work. We went to watch bands every Saturday night at the same bar, and we got recognized everywhere we went. It was a quaint area that was ridiculously cold in the winter. It's no surprise my first live shot was in a blizzard. Before I knew it, the year was up, and I was headed to my next stop.

Stop 2: Binghamton, New York—Market 154

It's here where I started to focus way too much on the future. I mean way too much. I was twenty-four years old and was trying to be the next Katie Couric. I couldn't cut myself a break and just breathe. I was hired as the 6:00 p.m. and 11:00 p.m. coanchor alongside a veteran in the industry, Steve Craig. The one cool thing about this gig is that we were on the city buses and a highway billboard. That doesn't happen all that often. However, I was an inexperienced anchor who should've been laser focused on being a great reporter first. I think I quickly started to realize that. I got bored living in another small city and not really getting a lot of live field experience. In order to make big moves early in this business, you need to be a solid reporter. I thought being a main anchor right away was the answer.

After a few months, I was already reaching out to Gary Brown in Providence, Rhode Island (market 53), along with a news director in Portland, Maine (market 80). I was dying to get back to New England, closer to family. I ended up getting a full-time offer in Portland before my contract was up. What was I thinking? You can't just break a contract because you want to go back home to a bigger market. That's not how it works, and it's a good way to tick people off. Why couldn't I just do what the rest of my colleagues in the industry were doing at that time? They knew they were there for two years. They enjoyed one another's company when the workday was over and kept in mind, "This is not a death sentence. This is temporary, and I'm going to enjoy every moment." I had a lot of fun with these people. I'm pretty certain none of them are in the business anymore, but they all went on to do good things. Anyway, what I'm saying is I should've just enjoyed the time there fully and not tried to cut corners.

The conversation did not go over well when I went to management and just assumed they were going to let me leave and go to Portland. Heck no. They said, "No. You have a contract, and we just plastered your face with Steve on highway billboards and buses." After a few months went by, they did what any management team would do. They found my replacement and told me, "Okay. We are not going to renew you since you clearly don't want to be here." I don't blame them one bit. I wasn't super upset, but I wasn't happy. I knew the Portland guy at least had me on his radar, as did Gary Brown in Providence. A friend of mine, Patrick, worked for Gary in Providence and told me to send him my résumé reel about a year before when I was still in Presque Isle. That's what started my rapport with Gary Brown, a very familiar name in the television news business.

Binghamton, New York highway billboard with Steve Craig

Stop 3: Providence, Rhode Island, and a Few
Other Occasional Freelance Stops

This now begins the "I eat, sleep, and breathe television news." My parents live an hour door-to-door to Providence with no traffic. When Gary took me on as a freelance reporter, he made it clear the hours would be all over the place and the shifts per week would be three. If someone was on vacation, there would be more. If no one was on vacation, there would be less. I remember many of those shifts being the early morning live reporter. That means being at work by 3:00 a.m. The morning show back then was from 5:00 a.m. to 9:00 a.m. This means you're live with a quick report every half hour. That's eight live shots, and it's not including live "coming up" teases at 5:00 a.m., 6:00 a.m., 7:00 a.m., and 8:45 a.m. Now, we're up to roughly twelve live shots per day. After that was done at around 9:15 a.m., I would go with the photographer to get some additional interviews and put together a report for the noon newscast. On occasion, we would go live at noon if it was a big story. The shift ended at 11:30 a.m., but I never said no to overtime because that would give them a reason to not keep me around as a freelancer and give the other ones more hours. So when all was said and done here, I was usually looking at a twelve-hour day. I would leave the house at 1:30 a.m. to get there by 2:45 a.m., work until 12:30 p.m., and get home by 1:30 or 2:00 p.m. I'm exhausted as I write this, thinking about how exhausted I must have been during those days. I remember just running on adrenaline. It was summer, and I STILL managed to find time (work hard, play hard) to have a social life and be well-prepared for my next shift.

To make ends meet financially, I was able to grab a shift or two a week at a cable station in Worcester, Massachusetts (a fifteen-minute drive), and also Derry, New Hampshire (a forty-five-minute drive). I needed to make sure I was working at LEAST four days a week. It was pretty stressful, but I was determined to do whatever it took to show Providence how willing I was to wait around for the first opening. There were some weeks where it ended up being a six- or seven-day workweek because I didn't want to say no to any of the stations who offered me hours. I also reached out to the station in Portland that offered me the reporter job I mentioned. A mentor/ acquaintance in the business told me the weekend anchor was going on maternity leave and the boss needed a temporary fill-in. He of course remembered me, and he gave me the gig. Fortunately, my great-uncle and aunt who adored me had a summer home in Maine. It was only a thirty-minute drive to the station. They graciously let me stay there on the weekends.

While this may seem like things were starting to fall into place, they were not. I was working tons of hours, driving all over creation, and getting nowhere. The boss in Portland called me after every newscast and criticized my anchoring. I knew deep down at twenty-four or twenty-five years old that I should be laser focused on finding a full-time reporter job, but I kept showing up and finished the six-week gig I had agreed to, thanked the boss, and became WAY too determined to stay in Providence. Finally, a full-time job was available. I thought for sure Gary was going to give me the gig. He didn't. He gave it to a woman who was working elsewhere and was a lot more qualified than I was. I didn't understand then, but I did later.

After a few days, I learned there was a weekend weather reporter opening. I immediately asked the morning meteorologist if he would teach me the weather. He said yes. I ran into Gary; and he said if I learned it and presented it well on tape, he would consider me. What the hell was I thinking? Really? I had zero interest in weather, yet I talked myself into spending hours and hours learning it JUST to be able to get a staff job here! I ended up doing a decent job presenting it on tape, but c'mon? I wouldn't and didn't stand a prayer up against a person who was already on television doing weather. As expected, she was hired. However, Gary proposed another idea. He put in a huge word at one of the group's sister stations in Toledo, Ohio. I was so disappointed, but I knew I wanted a REPORTER JOB WITH A NORMAL SCHEDULE FIVE DAYS A WEEK.

I'm all for people accepting an invitation for a job interview when you're seeking full-time employment. However, if it's a case where the company is paying for your flight and accommodations, you should only go if you're interested. At this point, I was. Not to mention, my college roommate and bestie, Deb, was living there at the time. We agreed if I accepted the gig, we would get an apartment together. I will cut to the chase. I went to the interview. I liked the boss. He liked me, and I was pretty sure I was going to get a firm offer. The day after I flew back home, he offered me the job, and I gave him a verbal yes over the phone. I told Deb I accepted, along with my other friends and family. We even had a going-away party at a local bar, and my dad's band played. The day the official contract was emailed and I had to sign it, I panicked. I couldn't sign it. I knew I wanted to stay in the Providence area. When I called the boss in Toledo to tell him, he was furious. It was mentioned in their local paper in "comings and goings" that I was hired. Not good. He then named off a couple of stations in the Boston market and told me, "I know people there, and I will let them know you did this. They will never hire you in the future." Fortunately, I did end up doing some work there, but that's not the point I'm trying to make. This flaky move I made caused me a lot of stress and ticked off a few people. Of course, add Gary to the list.

My next call was to him. He was not happy at all and told me, "Don't think we're going to allow you to freelance here anymore. Good luck."

My heart sank, and I thought, *What the hell have I done?*

I got some good advice from one of his anchors who said, "Yes, Gary is mad. He recommended you for that job. You're young. You made a stupid mistake. Don't do it again. However, don't waste time. Write and mail him an apology letter NOW." I took his advice. I spent a lot of time writing the letter. I never heard back. But I knew he was a reasonable guy and, at some point, we would cross paths.

I'm never one who really has immediate luck on her side. On this particular day, I did. It was probably a few days after the call to Gary. I went to the other two stations' websites in Providence and noticed the powerhouse station had a freelance opening. Yes, freelance—again—but YAY, PROVIDENCE! I sent an email to the bosses there and was upfront about the Toledo situation. They understood that I really wanted to be close to home and not twelve hours away. They told me to send my résumé reel. They ended up giving me the gig. This began another long cycle of all-over-the-place hours and never feeling like my life was in order.

Stop 4: Different Providence Station and Boston—Market 53 and Market 5 (Market 9 Now)

These days were some of the most exciting professionally. Nothing tops New York City; but being twenty-six to twenty-seven years old and working at the best station in Providence and then in Boston, a top-level market, (market 5 at the time) was too good to be true. It started out as a steady gig at this station in Providence. I was driving more than an hour to work and then back home at the end of long shifts. I loved it though. I got to report live at one of the Boston Red Sox World Series games and all the championship parades because Boston sports teams were all pretty amazing. This was all such a blast. Given the close proximity to Boston, the Providence stations would cover a lot of the same stories. This just fired me up to want to work in Boston even more, but I knew I wasn't quite ready.

I continued to work hard and ask for feedback. Some of it was good; some not so good. I wasn't exactly the best storyteller. I could get out the facts, present them live with confidence, but that was it. For example, covering a story in court where a suspect goes before a judge for allegedly stealing a stroller with a purse and a baby while that baby's mom turned her back for a split second to attend to her other child, a brand-new unpolished reporter would simply state the obvious: "Joe Jones showed no emotion as he learned his punishment today in court." A reporter with experience would tell a story and bring the viewer in by sharing an emotional story. "Every parent has their hands full with little children. This mother simply turned her back for one second, and police say Joe Jones saw a crime of opportunity. He ended up kidnapping a child all for a purse with ten dollars in it." You see my point. I'm forever grateful that the news director, Betty-Jo Cugini, took the time to explain this to me or at least wanted to help me improve. I wouldn't say I was the worst storyteller, but I did need improvement. With a lot of practice and feedback from Betty-Jo, it did get better. I was able to compile some really decent live shots and stories to put together a résumé reel. I went to my old stomping grounds at Boston University and dubbed some copies. Yes, I dubbed copy after copy. It was a grueling process. There was no emailing a link to your work at that time. I was sitting there, bored out of my mind, and I got a knock on the door. It was a sports journalism professor who remembered me. He told me my work looked really good. When he learned I was a freelancer at the NBC affiliate in Providence, he had mentioned there was a woman going on maternity leave at the NBC affiliate in Boston. He encouraged me to send this reel to the news director there. I didn't really think he was serious, but he was. I took his advice and sent it and thought nothing of it.

A few days later, I got a call from the news director who said he liked what he saw, but he wanted me to audition. I worked two weekend shifts for him, and he offered me the gig. However, the offer was under the assumption that my previous and current boss would recommend me. The first thing I thought of was Gary Brown. "What on earth would he say!" I was so nervous. I had no choice but to call him ASAP. I called his work number, and he answered. He said he had just received an email from the boss in Boston and hadn't yet replied. We spoke at length. We talked about how I bailed on Toledo. He was happy with the apology letter I had mailed and said it ticked him off to see me on the competing station in Providence a week later, but he understood. He said he would never jeopardize someone with work ethic, young age, and tenacity from reporting in the fifth largest market at a station my entire family watched. A few hours later, I was officially given the maternity leave gig. Life was great! Or so I thought!

The year 2005 was a roller coaster of emotions from excitement, thrill, nervousness, exhaustion, to disappointment. I will say it again. The freelance world is beyond unpredictable. When they say, "Jump," you say, "How high?" You really don't have a set schedule. I was guaranteed Saturday nights and Sunday mornings in Boston (that meant very little sleep in between), along with one day during the week. I was fortunate enough to have Betty-Jo in Providence plug me in for a day or two there, so I wouldn't be broke as a joke yet still keep my health benefits through the union there. However, I was still living out of a bag. I would stay at my parents' house, my boyfriend's in Boston, or at a friend's place. I toughed it out because I was so damn excited to be reporting in Boston. I couldn't even believe it. At twenty-six years old, I would be reporting at the station I watched growing up alongside people I looked up to and admired.

My excitement and work ethic were clearly noticed. Once the reporter out on maternity leave came back, they still kept putting me on the schedule. A few times, I was even live on MSNBC with some of the stories I did there. The first story was about houses being destroyed because of extreme flooding. I remember as clear as day saying to the photographer, John, "I'm beyond terrified to go live on national news! Help!"

He said, "Erin, you just did the live shot five minutes ago for the viewers in Boston. You're standing in the same spot with the same camera lens in front of you with the same photographer. You've got this." He was right. I put my big-girl pants on and knocked it out of the park because I was fired up.

The second scenario is absolutely hilarious, and it was in my hometown. I will never forget it. I was assigned a story about a cop on his way to serve an arrest warrant at a drug house when he gets badly bitten at the door by a squirrel. The picture in my head was priceless, with the buff officer getting his spot blown up by a tiny animal. I thought, *No effing way is he going to go on camera. The pressure was on. I'm being sent an hour away to my hometown. If I don't get this dude on camera, they will never put me on the schedule again.*

It will be O-V-E-R! (That's the other added pressure of a freelancer. You need to go above and beyond proving why they need to keep you around.) Sure enough, once we got to the police station and explained why we were there, the officers that came out laughed and said, "No way will Flowers go on camera about that! Good luck." After some serious begging, I got him to come out and talk to me. He refused an interview over and over again. I finally ended up getting through to him by explaining the story is actually quite funny; so let's just do this interview, share the story, and get on with our day. He caved. It was hilarious. The station loved the story. I went live from the kennel where the squirrel was "being held." My parents even came by to see the whole setup with the live shot and all the bells and whistles. That story also ended up on MSNBC. I'm guessing Officer Flowers regretted doing the interview, or maybe not.

A few more months went by of working crazy hours and being stressed to perform well every day with minimal sleep. I got wind that they were going to hire someone full-time who was an anchor/reporter from another station. I was so disappointed but was warned by a veteran reporter, "There are very few people who move from freelance to full-time once you show your willingness to work crazy, random hours. Why would station management hire you when they can hire someone else full-time yet still keep you on the schedule as needed?" I agreed. It made total sense. I immediately sent a résumé to Orlando, where some of my cousins live. Within a few weeks, I got the full-time gig. Once I accepted, I told management. They totally understood. It was a set schedule with steady pay and still in a top-twenty market. Looking back, this wasn't the best move. I sent one tape, got the gig, and accepted. I often wonder what would've happened if I had stuck it out a few more months as a freelancer and sent a few more tapes. I know. *Would've, could've, should've* is just a way of tormenting yourself. On a positive note, I now fully understood the value of hard work, being challenged, and being perceptive to feedback from true professionals. I respected people who worked hard every day. I walked away feeling well-prepared and ready for my next stop…or not?

Stop 5: Orlando—Market 18

I always imagined how much fun it would be to live in sunny Florida. It was fun—a lot of fun. I didn't love dripping sweat in my 5:00 p.m. live shots every day, and my hair was always a mess. But there was just something about the overall vibe there. The sunshine certainly put me in a better mood. I had my cousin Diane there, who's also my godmother, and her daughter, Debbie, who's just two years younger than me. It was great to reconnect with them and spend a lot of time together. Debbie and I had a ball going out in Orlando with her friends and my coworkers. I had a great apartment. You would think life would be wonderful.

I think at this point, age twenty-eight, is when I really started to wonder, *Am I just going to live all over the place?* All my close friends are getting married and have had only one maybe two jobs in their industry. A few months into my move here, I knew I had made an impulsive decision. My boyfriend from Boston and I had just broken up. The freelance schedule was killing me, and I wanted an escape. It's dumb to question that move now, but it's a lesson in impulsivity. The whole time I was there, I worked really hard, but I felt like I could never do a good-enough job. It was irritating because I knew where I stood at previous places. I couldn't seem to understand that not every manager is going to be forthcoming about what they feel is good, bad, and poor work. On the flip side, I didn't know there were some who wanted to find something wrong every single day with every single talent. Also, the style of reporting at one station can be completely different at another. Sometimes you have to suck it up and tweak a few words or sentences to the manager's liking and pick your battles. If you know deep down you're working hard and still being pushed to the limit where you don't have five seconds to eat or use the restroom, that's not good either. You need to figure out a way to do what's asked of you, do it well, yet still be kind to yourself. I don't know about you, but I don't do well on an empty stomach or a full bladder. I was kind of envious of the people who never let on to management that they were frustrated. In another sense, I was proud of those who really let them know. I was in the middle, yet the way I expressed it was a little on the insecure side. That's not good either. I put myself down, still busted my ass no matter what, and it just never got better. I was constantly trying to prove myself. Guess what? Not every gig in life is a perfect fit. Some managers, you will work great with, learn from, and respect even when they tell you what you don't want to hear. I LOVE those people. Two of them, I actually met here, but I didn't work long at all with them. One of them was on the front end. He loved my aggressiveness as a field reporter. He gave me advice on how to stand up for myself once he left, but he knew it would be a struggle in that environment. The other was a bit more mild-mannered and super intelligent. Even if he didn't like something, he would convey it politely and make it a teachable moment.

I met some phenomenal, talented reporters, photographers, and producers here. I will say we all seemed to have one another's backs, which is not always the case in this industry. There are so many moving parts in a newscast and even sometimes one simple story. If something goes wrong, you could easily point the finger at someone else. That didn't really happen. Many of us just wanted to do whatever it took to get through the day and not get a phone call from an upset manager. As my one-year mark approached, I knew this gig wasn't a good fit for me. That, coupled with the two-plus years of working crazy hours in Boston and Providence and living out of a bag, had me gravitating toward anchoring again. This would clearly mean a big drop in market size. At this point, nearing twenty-nine years old, making my job my life and fearing commitment with anything or any man, I'm giving myself permission to say it. I SHOULD'VE asked myself during this next three-year stint, "WHAT DO I REALLY, REALLY WANT?" I clearly really, really didn't know. I knew I still liked the business but started to really set the path in motion of "reporting facts and running from the truth."

Stop 6: South Bend—Market 88 at the Time

Since I already informed you in chapter 1 of the "nightmare" part of my final days in South Bend, I will make this part short. Many people have said/asked me, "This has got to be the one stop along the way that you regret." Not true at all. I got three years of Monday-to-Friday anchoring experience alongside two people who had twenty-plus years' experience at the anchor desk. The news director also really liked me. He chose me and had gone back and forth with my agent at the time about the job title and pay. He gave me what we had asked for. I was the 5:30 p.m. coanchor, and I also reported for the 11:00 p.m. news. I didn't love the reporting aspect of it because I had recently reported in Orlando and Boston, which are top-twenty news markets. However, I made the most of it and made sure my delivery in the field was solid. It was my name and my face signing off in the report, and I'm not a half-assed person. The challenge was always getting done anchoring at 6:00 p.m. and getting out the door with a photographer to go shoot videos and get interviews for my reporter assignment, then writing it, having him edit the story, and then going live at 11:00 p.m. It sounds exhausting, and it was. But a part of me enjoyed the adrenaline rush. It was even wilder on the nights the 11:00 p.m. anchors were off. I would anchor at 5:00 p.m./5:30 p.m./6:00 p.m., bundle up, go out and file a report, rush back, write it, change clothes again, and prepare for the 11:00 p.m. newscast.

It was very difficult to find a group of friends to hang with in this market. I was twenty-nine or thirty and all the other reporters were in their early twenties. The other anchors were in their forties and married with children. Fortunately, I am very social, and in no time, I met some people from the area. It was easy to do when Notre Dame football season kicked off shortly after I moved to town! I will tell you. Out of all the places I've lived, I never had more visitors than I did in South Bend. We had a ball at all the football and basketball games. If it were an away game or off-season, we would take the train to Chicago and split a hotel room. My friends who visited also enjoyed meeting some of the local people I befriended. Over the course of three years, there was a lot of fun to be had.

It was here where I also learned the importance of networking and taking advantage of your surroundings. I was working steps away from the University of Notre Dame. I thought, *How great would that be to say I did some type of public speaking instruction of sort there?* I met some really impressive people who worked there. Someone had mentioned, "With your background, you should reach out to the business school and see if they need any assistance with media training for students. A lot of them are great at analyzing scenarios and knowing how to defend their [future] company in a crisis scenario on paper but not when hounded by a reporter with a microphone." I took the advice, reached out, and was able to do just that a few times a year. In fact, even two months after being cleared from my arrest (again, no charges filed), Marc Hardy, a professor in nonprofit executive leadership, allowed me to come back and teach a three-day seminar in crisis communication to about thirty people from the United States Hispanic Chamber of Commerce. The attendees ranged in age from late twenties to late sixties. I absolutely loved this experience. I felt confident, relaxed, and proud of myself. Oh, and did I mention how great the pay was? I guess the group of thirty liked me too. I got an overall score of 4.5 out of 5 with a three-day lesson plan I crafted all on my own. I also made some great connections and friends. To this day, I have kept in contact with Marc. He's not only been a true friend but a mentor and a great person to have listed on my résumé as a reference. If I ever get out of TV news, I've always said I would love to start a business of some sort with him whether it be a speaking/consulting thing or lead a nonprofit.

Before I started doing these gigs at Notre Dame, I had already done some adjunct teaching at Indiana University South Bend. One course was in mass communications, and the other was in business communications. I really enjoyed this, but it made for a very LONG day. I would get up, get ready, cook my meals for the day, teach, and go to work. I kept really focused and busy during the workweek and looked forward to having fun on the weekends. I will say this. Working until 11:30 p.m. Monday to Friday at thirty years old is not ideal for having a social life. I wasn't going to go to a bar after work to meet people. Plus, I had to be well-rested for these long days ahead for teaching, anchoring, and reporting. It seems like all was going well, right? I was so over-the-top busy and jam-packed my schedule that even if I wasn't happy, I was too tired to think about it. I had so many distractions to keep me busy, focused, and excited for the FUTURE. I clearly wasn't just enjoying the present. I remember going to bed thinking about what may be my next big career move. I knew I had until April 2010 on my contract in South Bend.

I already explained in chapter 1 how I fell apart and how three FULL years of hard work ended. To recap the facts, I was two weeks from completing a job well done here. I started at the end of April 2007. In mid-April 2010, it all blew up in my face. For nearly a year and a half leading up to that day, I was running on empty, constantly sad and wanting a relationship to work that wasn't and simply tormenting the hell out of myself. If only I realized that things were not nearly as bad as they seemed. Not even close.

Stop 7: Providence, Rhode Island... Again!

This now means I've officially been on air at all three stations in the market! Crazy, but not really. I liked all the people I previously worked with in Providence from talent to photographers, producers, and management. I'm glad I worked hard and left a good impression on the managers at the two other stations because I can promise you this third station made some calls and asked around. I was hired as a full-time reporter and fill-in anchor in June 2010, two months after the South Bend incident. BJ Finnell was the news director and Steve Doerr was the general manager. Right now in 2020, I told Steve I was finally ready to put out my story of self-doubt and torment in order to help others. He sent me this statement dated in October.

> Logan's "comeback," if you want to call it that, began in my office. It was the summer of 2010, a few months after the shit show in South Bend. She was trying to restart her career by coming home to New England and I was running a TV station in Providence that needed to add talent. Logan—nobody who knows her well calls her Erin—hit a lot of brick walls at the beginning. The South Bend incident was well known inside the TV industry. The TV News gossip sites wrote about it ad nauseam and had a picnic with the

juicy nuggets: THREE INCH STILETTOS! A
NOTRE DAME/CHICAGO BEARS STAR!
And that mug shot? DAMN! But tabloid or not, it
was a thing. Many stations wouldn't touch her. And
Logan felt every bit of it deeply. It was crushing.

One of my core management strategies is
to find over-qualified people who need a second
chance. Yes, it's a decent thing to do but candidly
it's also smart business. Over the years I've hired
a lot of people who, for various, often tabloidy
reasons, need another shot. These people are the
best value in TV. They're enormously talented
but they've been humbled. They're driven to
prove the haters wrong. They're fiercely loyal.
Logan's talent is obvious. Just look at her resume
reel and you'll see it—hell, you can't miss it. But
I needed to know if she had the emotional IQ to
not only do the job, but to heal. Because to be
the kind of colleague we needed her to be, we
needed her to be healthy. She lost everything—
her career, her reputation, her privacy—was she
strong enough to fight through the PTSD and
leverage that enormous talent? We wanted to
know so we brought her in to talk.

She walked into my office and locked eyes—
Logan's eyes are piercing and green and she uses
them very effectively; she reached out and shook
my hand, firmly and confidently. I invited her
to sit down and tell me the story. And she did.
She owned it. No excuses, no qualifications. But
she added detail and context, which I know firsthand matters enormously. She rounded out the
story. My conclusion? It was clear that she was
damaged, but it was equally clear that she was
strong. Strong enough to make it to the other

side I offered her the job and "after" part—as in before and after "the incident"—began.

Logan thrived professionally but was still not able to get past it. The TV News gossip cycle rolled along and the thing in Indiana faded from memory, but Logan didn't let it go. She couldn't—and she knew it. Every time she'd meet someone new, she wondered if they "knew." She was allowing it to define her. We talked about it directly. I told her she needed to move forward with her head up or have her life defined by something that lived primarily in her own head and in any event, it couldn't be changed. Intellectually, she knows that but even now, almost eleven years later, it haunts her. But I think the light switch has gone on. In the summer of 2020, in the midst of the COVID pandemic, I heard a change in Logan's tone. She had decided to share her story with others who may be allowing ghosts from the past to shade the future. I told her I could sense it and she agreed. She had finally come to terms with it and it was time for her next act. Over the years we talked about: address it, fix it and move on. Logan finally had. (Steve Doerr, VP general manager, Meredith Broadcasting)

I'm forever grateful to Steve and BJ for looking past the "tabloid" articles and doing their own investigation on who I was/am as a person and my abilities as a journalist. As Steve said back then, "The charges were dropped. You don't have a record. You weren't in public, and it was one bad night." I was so excited to now be one hour from home and working in a market that was very familiar. I found an amazing apartment right on Federal Hill, which is the Little Italy of Providence. It's a street filled with amazing restaurants and cute shops.

I remember barely sleeping the few nights before my first day. I called BJ and said, "I don't think I can do this. I'm not ready. What if people who see me on air send video clips to the TV gossip sites and people start bashing me again?"

He said, "Are you kidding? We just gave you this opportunity, and you're going to let a bunch of haters win?"

I immediately agreed, apologized, and the conversation was two minutes long. I showed up on my first day with my head held high. I ended up interviewing my close friend's husband, who was a state senator. I felt at ease until it was 5:00 p.m. live shot time. I did fine, but inside I felt like a scared child. When I went back to the station, I could sense the awkwardness from some people. One of the photographers had clued me in that BJ held a meeting a few days before and told the staff that if anyone was caught talking about the South Bend incident in the newsroom and made me feel unwelcome, that they would be getting a call from him. I did in fact catch a few people as expected, but I didn't go tattle to BJ. It is what it is. I knew in time they would see I was a tenacious journalist who got the job done and was also fun to be around.

I knew things would eventually get better. On DAY 2, BJ and Steve let me fill in for the female evening anchor who was out sick. I knew they knew I could do it based on my three-year evening anchor gig in South Bend. I just assumed they wouldn't put me at the desk for at least a few months. I ended up fill-in anchoring quite a bit for the fourteen months I worked there. I worked Monday through Friday nights until 11:30 p.m. I didn't care what my schedule was at this time. I was just so excited to be back on air AND able to see my close friends and family. I loved digging for sources and getting exclusive interviews, and I really enjoyed seeing my old colleagues in the field and making new lasting friendships.

This was a third-place station in the Providence market. In this case, it made the job a little more exciting for the reporters. Shannon and Mark—I can't even count the amount of hours we spent thinking of story ideas, meeting new contacts, and, most importantly, enjoying one another's company. We laughed. We cried, and we were excited to go to work every day at the third-place station. The pay wasn't ideal, but we took pride in our work. We had all previously worked in bigger markets. I was a reporter in Orlando and Boston. Mark was an anchor in San Francisco, and Shannon was a reporter in Cleveland. For one reason or another, we all ended up working together in Providence, all hired by Steve. The station ended up being sold to another company, so Steve and BJ left. I ended up getting a new job a few months later in New Haven, Connecticut. It was a bigger market, more money, and a great opportunity.

Stop 8: New Haven, Connecticut—Market 29 at the Time

It's now early September 2011. This means we're nearing a year and a half since the South Bend nightmare and on to my second job. Clearly, all of the managers here and in Providence were not hung up on what happened because it was ridiculous and over. It wasn't over though for some of my new colleagues at the station and others in local media. That meant it definitely wasn't over for me as I was still in a pathetic pattern of letting other people's opinion of me ruin my day.

I will never forget one of my first few days. I was working the most difficult shift as the morning live reporter. Once again, up at about 1:30 a.m., at work by 3:00 a.m., and live on television ten-plus times. I heard there was a local gossip site about the media a few days before. I stupidly looked at it in between live shots. There it was! The ridiculous South Bend mug shot as my "Welcome to Connecticut." People were of course commenting. I swear I loved tormenting myself. I couldn't wait until after my shift to read the tabloids. I immediately started crying and thought, *Here we effing go again!* The poor photographer, Kevin, had no clue what to say or do other than be kind, keep it real, and help me get it together in the short ten minutes before the next live shot. I got through it, and we chatted. He told me what I already knew. There are always going to be people who LOOOVE to see others fall and make mistakes. It's how you recover and present yourself. Again, I was already two jobs post-South Bend in a top-thirty market at a great station and close to family.

I did what I did in Providence. I showed up with a smile on my face, worked my butt off, showed I took the job seriously, yet still had a sense of humor during downtime. Some of the staff came around pretty fast and welcomed me; others did not. The people who asked questions about the incident, I gladly told. Others, I felt I had to explain myself before they would ever give me the time of day. I accepted that not everyone is going to like and accept me and that's life. For the most part, I made a ton of friends here. I still talk to Kevin often and a few others who watched me cry a few times and certainly laugh often. If you're stuck in a live truck all day with someone, you get to know a lot about them.

After a year, I was offered the weekend anchor/reporter job. That meant I reported three days a week, was off Thursdays and Fridays, and anchored the weekend nights. I was also part of the investigative unit. When the main anchors were off, I also filled in for them. I was paid decent money. I was at a great station, but yes, no one really wants to work weekend nights long term. I did it for nearly three years. I made the most of it as Thursdays and Fridays are not bad nights to have off. When early 2013 hit and I had this new role as anchor / reporter / investigative reporter, why couldn't that have been the end of the self-torment regarding South Bend? I know Steve Doerr mentioned that it should've been over the second he hired me in Providence. Personally, I wanted a gig that included anchoring and reporting in at least a top-fifty market (this was thirty then) to make me feel better. I officially had just that, so why did this self-doubt continue? I can say now it's because I let this career define me. I put it first. This is all I had other than my parents and best friends. I had entertained serious relationships but was afraid that I wouldn't be able to have both. I think that's why I gravitated toward men who weren't a good match for me. Also, I often thought, *Who would want to date me if I wasn't on TV?* How sad is that?

I spent more than four years at this New Haven station and signed three contracts here. I was/am proud of the work I did here, but these four years (and a few more after) were wildly spent "reporting facts and running from the truth." All I cared about was being successful and proving people wrong. I thought I wanted to settle down. I thought I was a loser because I hadn't found my match. I didn't have children, a house, or tons of money. I thought my head was going to explode. I was again becoming my own worst enemy.

In 2015, while engaged/unengaged, I still continued to do my job and did it well. I was just sad all the time and letting my personal life affect my mood. I tried to keep it on the down low, but c'mon. People notice and overhear conversations. Oh, and once you tell one or two coworkers something, it often becomes like a game of telephone. At this point, I had been hired by one news director here, promoted by another, kept around by a third, and a fourth had just been hired. I could tell off the bat he wasn't a huge fan. I think he liked my work, but looking back, I'm sure he could tell I was miserable. When my contract was coming to an end and I hadn't heard anything, I started looking around at other stations in the market. There was an opening, but the timing was off by about two months. I knew this current boss wasn't going to renew me, so I was prepared. I got lucky because the other station did have another opening.

Stop 9: Still Connecticut but Hartford

If I can say one thing and one thing only, I struck gold with bosses here. The general manager, Jon Hitchcock, welcomed me with open arms. Oh, and the boss who hired me in New Haven, John Bell, was now working here. This meant I would be working closely with him during my reporter shifts. I had missed the first anchoring opportunity a few months back because I was still under contract in New Haven. Hitchcock told me to bear with him as there would be another opening around the corner. So for the first few months, I reported Monday through Friday, 9:30 a.m. to 5:30 p.m., the hours people in the business would kill for. I hated it because of my one-hour-traffic commute to work and then an hour-plus home. I also missed the anchoring aspect. Within three months, Jon delivered. He offered me the weekend morning anchor gig. That meant I would report three days a week, off Thursday and Friday, and anchor a three-hour show from 6:00 a.m. to 9:00 a.m. on Saturdays and Sundays. My shift started at 4:30 a.m. on the weekend, which meant I was up at 2:30 a.m. because of the drive. It sounds nuts, but it wasn't bad at all. And I preferred it over the five-days-a-week reporting. I got a lot done on my off days, and I could still meet people for an early dinner on weekends or really any night of the week. The people were really nice to work with just as they were in New Haven. The gig worked for me for a short time, but then the "I feel like a loser" attitude kicked in again. I took steps to address this inner battle of incredibly low self-worth and self-doubt as I describe in detail in chapter 7. I ended up completing my full year here and decided I needed a change. I made a bold move by leaving a job without another set in stone, but it ended up working out. Well, at least for an additional sixteen months. A few days later, I got a freelance gig in New York City. I truly wish I had stayed a little bit longer here and been more committed to a boss who was more than kind to me. Freelance gigs in big markets pop up more often than you would think.

Hartford, Connecticut

Stop 10: New York City—Market 1

When offered this gig in late December 2016, I was ecstatic. I was ecstatic about it even when told, "Nothing is guaranteed. Some people last just a few shifts—others a few weeks, months, or years. We take it day by day." I didn't care. I knew when given the chance that I would do just fine like I did eleven years before in my late twenties as a freelancer in Boston. Only this time, the whole picture seemed much, much bigger. This was market 1, and the newsroom was in the CBS Broadcast Center.

The start of this gig sort of reminded me of the one in Boston. I was paired up with a photographer named Jim Duggan who put me at ease. Just like the photographer in Boston, he said, "Do it like you've been doing it. It's just a camera lens you're looking into." I agreed.

But I wanted so badly to keep getting put on the schedule, so fear of error was always on my mind. I will say. Not being from the area, it was difficult to categorize specific locations and points of reference in certain stories, but I always double-checked with someone before saying it on air. For a top market, it was like a breath of fresh air to see how easygoing and welcoming people were. Even reporters at other stations were really cool when we were on the same story.

The sixteen months I spent here were great. I was excited, challenged, but running on fumes. The first few months, my schedule was allllll over the place. I spent so much money staying in hotels because I was living in Connecticut. When I worked the early morning shift, there was no train, and I didn't feel safe driving that far in the middle of the night to NYC alone. Once I had somewhat of a predictable schedule, it was still a very long day—on the train at 6:55 a.m. for an hour, then take a cab or another train from Grand Central Station to the West Side. There were times I would barely make it in time for the 9:00 a.m. meeting, and boy, did I look like an idiot walking in late. It was already nerve-wracking trying to find story ideas to pitch in that meeting with all the managers and your colleagues staring. That was always one of the scariest parts of the day for me and the other freelancers. You looked bad and unprepared if your idea wasn't great. After getting home from work most nights at 8:30 p.m. or 9:00 p.m. because of the long commute, I would try like hell to keep my eyes open and search for ideas on the train. Sometimes it worked; sometimes it didn't. I did myself no favors living so far away.

No matter what the assignment was or how tired I was, I made sure to give it my all by digging for details, asking the right questions on scene, playing detective, and most importantly, being personable to potential interviewees. I didn't have a lot of trouble getting people to welcome me into their home to be interviewed. I loved putting the story together under pressure and running in front of the camera to go live. When working weekends, you have a very short window to gather interviews and go live at 6:00 p.m. when you're getting out the door at 4:00 p.m. We did it though. There were a few F bombs in the live truck followed by laughs. There was pressure to do the job and do it well, but everyone was good in their roles.

The second most stressful part of my day makes everyone laugh. You ready? I was shaking every time I would voice or "track" my story. That should actually be a reporter's least stressful thing to do. The hard part is over. You've gathered interviews. Your story is written, and it's been approved by a manager. All you have to do is read it from the paper for the editor. It sounds simple—read from the paper. Yes, but read with inflection, emotion, slow down, speed up. I just sounded flat and boring and COMPLETELY different than when I was reporting LIVE in the field or studio. It made no sense that I just kept sounding dull. It was so frustrating for me and even more frustrating for the managing editor, Dan. His boss was getting annoyed; and Dan was my direct supervisor, along with all the other reporters. Before any of our stories made air, Dan would go watch it and approve it in the edit bay. That means the days when I wasn't live in the field, I would be sitting in the edit bay with the editor, watching Dan watch my story. I swear my blood pressure would be sky-high when I saw him walking by. One of the editors, Vinny, used to try and make me laugh by saying things like "Oh boy, here he comes. I think he will like the tracking today." It was the worst feeling on the days he didn't. That's because all the hard work of putting the story together, he would applaud. It was the stupid voicing that irked him.

It may sound strange, but I miss the no-room-for-error, double-checking-work management style. Even people who've been doing this for thirty years make random little mistakes. One wrong word could get a station sued. I'm a perfectionist; and I tend to like, appreciate, and admire people who expect great work and push you to make it happen. It's been nearly three years now and not a day goes by that I don't think of Dan when I track a story. It's much, much better, even the consultant recently gave me a compliment. Still, there's something about me reading "live" that sounds much better. It's okay. No one is perfect at every single part of their job. We can all improve.

Just like Boston, freelance gigs run their course. They wear on you, and they're not stable. I wasn't living in New York, and more local reporters from other New York City stations were being added to the schedule. They had a HUGE advantage over me. They knew how to shoot and edit their own stories, and they knew their way around the area. The station was training all the full-timers to learn to shoot video, and many of them were being required to go out by themselves once a week to do just that. I was the only freelancer who never had to do this in previous jobs, so I knew my days were numbered when I never offered to learn. They politely told me they couldn't put me on the schedule anymore. I understood. and it was amicable. Any reporter who shoots and edits in a small town they're familiar with will tell you it makes for a loooong day. I wouldn't have survived a minute doing this in NYC.

This experience was awesome. I'm so glad I did it and grateful to have worked alongside so many top-notch managers and talent in the industry. The main anchor, Dana Tyler, couldn't have been nicer. I was just one of the many circulating freelancers; and she always gave me feedback, including applauses and areas to improve.

New York City

Stop 11: Cleveland—Market 19

I guess I was meant to end up living in Ohio close to my bestie, Deb, at some point during my adventurous career. Remember, that was the plan/idea when I got the job offer in Toledo in 2004. Fast-forward to summer 2018. I hadn't seen her in person since she had her son, Nicholas, who was now about to turn three years old. When I told her I had an interview in Cleveland, her hometown, she was excited. She met me at the hotel I was staying at near the TV station, and we talked for hours and hours. She was hopeful I would get the job and accept.

I made my intentions clear to management that I was a little burned out from spending hours on end in live trucks all day every day; but I absolutely wanted to still report in some capacity every day, as well as anchor at least one show. They understood and said they would come up with something. I was really hoping I would not be working five nights a week given my age and the fact that I was single and moving to a brand-new city where I knew no one but Deb and her husband. She's a married woman with a child and is a doctor. Clearly, I knew I wouldn't get to see her like old times. I figured the best way to meet people would be after work during the week, perhaps at the dinner hour or at philanthropic events. That didn't happen at all, at least not during the first full year.

I was offered the job as the Monday to Friday 10:30 p.m. anchor/reporter and accepted. This means my schedule was 3:30 p.m. to 11:30 p.m. I was happy I would be anchoring five times a week but a little disappointed about the hours for the above reasons. I definitely had good reason. Almost everyone at the station was married, so it was tough to meet friends. The ones who were married or had significant others worked a day shift and got out of work by 6:00 p.m., and on weekends, they were with their families.

I also had a few targets on my back which led people to not be overly friendly in the beginning. I had recently worked in NYC (a bigger market, 1 versus 19). I had previously worked for the general manager of this station and was hired by him and a fairly new news director. That's not all. People, myself included, were confused by this strange anchor time slot I was given—a half-hour solo show from 10:30 p.m. to 11:00 p.m. It gave the two evening anchors a short break, but the timing was strange. After just two months, it was announced that the 4:00 p.m. and 6:00 p.m. anchors were leaving at the end of the year. Immediately, everyone assumed I would be doing the 4:00 p.m. and the primary evening anchors would take over the 6:00 p.m. For a month or two in the interim, people were even more standoffish. I don't mean just other anchors or reporters who wanted the job. It was just a mix of people who assumed I was the golden child because of who hired me. Well, that didn't happen at all. They ended up promoting the woman who was doing the noon show. She had been there at least three years and did a great job. I was not at all upset with her as she deserved it. I was just upset that the bosses hadn't really tipped me off when I signed my contract that there were other people ahead of me they were considering should more anchoring become available. I mean I guess I never directly asked that question before signing, nor did they really have to give a new employee that answer. I of course assumed the worst. *I'm not doing a good enough job or else they would've given me that gig. I mean, primary anchors never leave, and I just missed this opportunity. It's over. There will never be another one during this three-year contract!* I was so upset, and I asked if I could just leave since it had only been four months. I stated pretty much what I just said above. "I'm clearly not doing a good job in your eyes, and an opportunity like this is not going to come up again." They asked me to be patient and said, "Let's talk again in a few months about potential role changes." That was in early January 2019.

Over the next few months, people started to be more welcoming now that they saw firsthand I wasn't the golden employee who would be given special treatment. Some even told me they felt bad that I didn't get the promotion. I wouldn't say all of them went out of their way to include me in conversations at work in the newsroom. However, some did, and they were really nice. I made the most of these cold, dreary winter months trying to keep busy when not at work. When I was at work, I tried my best to do good stories with limited resources. There were many times I didn't have a photographer; so I just stayed at the station and put something together for someone to edit and then stand in front of the camera to report the story live in the studio. I also made sure I did a good job anchoring the 10:30 p.m. It can be challenging when alone; but I took full advantage of the entertainment segment where they let the meteorologist, Jason, also my friend, coanchor with me. A lot of it, we ad-libbed. It was hilarious to the point we would try and throw people's names in like our buddy, Tim, who we knew was watching. We said, "Oh, look at John Travolta. He kind of looks like local Realtor, Timothy Damiano." It showed I was a real person and not just someone reading a prompter. Our bosses liked it, as well as the station's consultant.

A few months later, July 2019, the Major League All-Star Game was held in Cleveland. The male anchor was off, so they had me fill in with the main female anchor, Tiffani. It was a blast anchoring live outside Progressive Field. Nearly all of it was ad-libbed, so I took full advantage. I remember walking away thinking, *Wow, Tiffani and I had good chemistry*. Also, Jason and Sam, the meteorologists, and Tony, the sports director, were with us, so it made it even better. I think management agreed.

One month later, I was offered the 5:00 p.m. and 5:30 p.m. time slot with Tiffani. No one lost their jobs. Management just shuffled the lineup and included me. There's another added bonus! I would be working 10:30 a.m. to 6:30 p.m.! Those are the best hours in television news. The gig was set to start in September, a few days after my one-year anniversary. I thought, *FINALLY, my hard work is being noticed, and I get to work hours that will allow me to have a life*.

I can honestly say from September 2019 up until nightmare COVID in March 2020, things were pretty darn good. Those six months seemed way too good to be true. I got to go to the gym before work and still get things done at night or even meet someone for dinner. I was making new friends, and I became really hopeful that things were going to start falling into place. I really enjoyed anchoring with Tiffani, and the show was doing well. Most importantly, I wasn't living in the past anymore. Now, that I felt comfortable professionally and personally, I decided to think about working on the other aspect of my life that I put on the burner for so long—dating and relationships. At the very least, I was ready to at least give men a chance if it was someone I found interesting or if a friend wanted to introduce me to someone. Well, that idea didn't last. COVID shut the world down.

During my first year in Cleveland, I learned to embrace my alone time and relaxing. There were times when I could've gone out but chose to stay home and do other things. Thank goodness, or I would've been in for an even ruder awakening. For anyone else out there who is living alone with no family close by, I feel for you. This pandemic has been very lonely—sometimes so lonely all you have time to do is sit around thinking how lonely you may be for the rest of your life. I kept thinking, *What if I had no family to at least call? What if when I'm sixty-five years old, I'm still sitting here single?* It was tough, but I kept busy. Deb invited me over almost every weekend, and I grew close to her now five-year-old son. I powered through. I still am. Even though businesses are back open, it's not very exciting as you very well know. All we can do is go get a meal and ONLY interact with people at our table.

I feel fortunate that my job has kept me busy. I'm still able to work every day, though that has had its challenges. For the first few months, March to July, I was able to at least work at the station and not from home. Regardless, this whole situation has piled on the workload for everyone. The producers have to write a show for two anchors who aren't even in the same room or building. One is at home, and one is at the studio. Talk about nonstop opportunities for communication breakdown! Everyone has pulled their weight and done a great job through it all.

During this time, I have/had been really stressed out. I'm not going to lie. My schedule was changed from noon to 8:00 p.m. because management needed me to coanchor the 7:30 p.m. with my friend, Tony Zarrella. He's a fellow Bostonian, and our east coast roots made it easy to form an instant friendship from day 1. Anyway, I was excited about coanchoring with him, but this added a lot more work on my plate. When I started at noon, I would link up with a photographer who was off the clock at 3:00 p.m. This meant I had to drive in my own car (COVID policy) to meet him to gather interviews, write the story, hand it to him for him to edit it, and be out the door by 3:00 p.m. Then, I had a minute to breathe, get a cup of coffee, read the 5:00 p.m. to 6:00p.m. show and make any necessary changes, speak briefly with Tiffani and Heather (our producer) about the show, fix my hair and makeup, do a live studio appearance at 4:00 p.m., and then anchor the big show with Tiffani from 5:00 p.m. to 6:00 p.m. Then, I had a dinner break and prepared for the 7:30 p.m. The days certainly blew by, which I liked, but the drive to work and the worry about getting to the photographer on time to get the story done in a short window was nerve-wracking.

Once late summer hit, I was asked to work from home, which I was not at all thrilled about. However, to make it fair, they wanted all the anchors to take turns from home every other week. I was terrified because I'm not very experienced with the latest and greatest TV technology. Also, my coanchor, Tiffani's husband is a photographer and was there to help her set up, and if something went wrong, he was there to fix it. The other female anchor's husband was also there to help her, and the male anchor was already well-versed with technology. I expressed my fears/concerns, and management understood what I was up against. I gave it my all and just said to myself, "Do your best on air. Everyone else has had technical errors at home, and viewers are aware we are working from home at this time." I rolled with it, and there were some good shows and not-so-good shows. There's no teleprompter at home, so I feel this forced me to be even more animated. It was strange to have to memorize someone else's stories, so I tried to read it in a more conversational tone. It was already awkward enough having a tiny, little pinhole on an iPad as my camera! So I controlled what I could control—my delivery.

After two months, they told me I didn't have to work from home anymore because the signal from where I lived was not reliable. There were too many glitches. You can't have constant technical problems during a 5:00 p.m. broadcast. At this point, I had kind of gotten used to some of the benefits of working from home. You can wear sweatpants 'cause no one sees them, and you control your workday up until airtime. I was fine either way. However, a new curveball was thrown at me just last week in September. I was told I would no longer have a photographer or editor, so I would need to learn how to edit my own stories at the station. So I have to learn how to edit. I thought, *I can barely get the report done between noon and three WITH a photographer/editor in this short window!* They explained I would just gather elements from stories already shot by a photographer or put together a national story. Sometimes this can stall you a bit because you weren't the one gathering the elements, so it's like you're starting from scratch. Still, I knew that was my strength, and that wasn't the issue. The issue was having to then EDIT in an hour or so when I've never ever edited a frame of video in my life other than VHS tape to tape in 2002 in Presque Isle, Maine. I knew nothing about nonlinear editing. It actually terrified me.

After a lot of complaining (not refusing) and extensive practice, I've been editing on my own for a few weeks now. They've been giving me assignments like they said they would, simple and ready to start when I walk in at noon to start my shift. I'm not great at it, but I'm getting the job done. I look at it as learning a new skill. I'm a little bummed though that I can't go out and do my own stories and do what I love—gathering elements and interviewing people. Now, I don't leave the building. I know everyone's work routine has changed since the start of the pandemic. I wish I hadn't been as vocal about having to learn how to edit. I'm pulling it off as I knew I would. The first three hours of my shift are even more nerve-wracking! However, it's teaching me that they're not expecting any award-winning reports from me under the circumstances. They even made it clear they consider me more of an anchor.

I have no idea what the future holds. I'm happy to say that last month on my two-year anniversary, I was told by the news director and assistant news director that they would like to keep me around longer and to start thinking about contract negotiations much earlier than the ending of my current one in September 2021. I was very excited, and it made me feel relaxed. I'm living in the present and focusing on one day at a time. I guess that's the one good thing a pandemic has taught me—be thankful for every single day and deal with the ups and downs as they come. Worrying about editing? Please.

Cleveland, Ohio

Cleveland, Ohio
with Tony Zarrella
outside First
Energy Stadium

Lessons Learned, Laughs Shared, and Tears Shed throughout the Journey

There's no short list of adjectives to describe this wild journey. Wow. While writing this chapter, I felt every single emotion possible. I realized how blessed I am, how dedicated and passionate I am about the work I do, and how many invaluable lessons I've learned about myself and people in general. This is a very difficult profession to get into without a little bit of help from family in the beginning. It's very difficult to make ends meet making twenty to forty thousand dollars, especially if you're a woman on television. More than half of your paycheck is spent on clothes, hair, and makeup. I've had very few jobs where the station covered a lot of those costs. However, finances are just a small part of the equation. I never would've made it through without my parents, grandparents, and friends as my personal cheerleaders. Being told to cut your hair, dye your hair, find a foundation that masks your freckles better, and the pressure to be in shape and look great all the time can be exhausting. Some women make this the center of their world. I was one of them. I spent A LOT of time worrying about how I looked while anchoring the news. There are a few nights I remember clearly when I could barely read because I was paranoid that I didn't look good enough. Some idiot in Connecticut used to write in about my crooked eyebrow and would start discussions on social media about this. I would spend so much time doing my eyebrows in the makeup room. Then, after the newscast, I would go back and watch it to see if the eyebrows were okay. REALLY? If someone is going to watch or not watch because they don't like one of my eyebrows, that's crazy. That's nothing. The real challenge is learning to go about your daily life without worrying what your fans, haters, and creepers choose to say about you. It will happen no matter how big or small of a city you live in, especially in today's world where your every move could be under a microscope. You need thick skin—period. Or you will fall apart. I know many others in different professions also have to deal with this aggravation. Don't let it control your day. Please.

I hope my lessons learned about showing commitment translate to you or perhaps anyone you know. It's not right to lead a potential employer on and tell them you want the job when you know deep down that's not the case. Make sure you're committed. Finish the contract on good terms, and move on to the next gig. Cutting corners to move ahead can be exciting and rewarding, but it never really lasts. You get burned out, and it's not a sure thing. If you're married or have a very secure source of income, then freelance or temporary gigs might be a great thing. I don't recommend this in the beginning of a career. That's just my two cents. Enjoy the present and know these contracts are not forever if you don't want them to be. Being ambitious and thinking ahead is good but only if you find a middle ground.

Someone once said to me that good management will build a team that is like a "cast of characters where everyone is a little bit different." I've definitely seen this at many stations, and it's really important. Everyone brings something a little bit different to the table. I always tried to find certain skills in people I admire, and I still do. No matter how experienced you are or think you are in a profession, there's always an opportunity to learn something from others. Be humble, be helpful, and be respectful. My biggest pet peeve is arrogance. No one is better than anyone. Period. You may not choose to pal around with some of your coworkers outside of work, but purposely excluding people at large group gatherings is just childish. Some stations would have going-away parties for people and only send an email inviting a select few. I was always taught when you bring a bunch of cookies or cupcakes to class or work, you bring enough for everyone. You may not like some of the people, but what harm does it do by simply being cordial? Also, you never know how someone really is unless you give them a chance. Some of the people who I thought I would never hit it off with, I ended up enjoying the most. Some who I thought were my friends were the ones who stabbed me in the back. It's nice to have friends at work, but you don't need to tell these people your personal business. It took me years to figure this out. Now I know for certain who my real friends are in this business, and I'm blessed because they are phenomenal people. As for management, I've given examples of learning how to adapt to different styles. Pick your battles. When things start to become unbearable, ask a loved one's opinion before making any drastic moves. If things don't change, then you know what to do. Oh, and if you have a boss who you know believes in you, likes you as a person, and has your back, be thankful. I've had quite a few, and they know who they are.

All of my coworkers and bosses, along with my former ones, know that this job is certainly not a Monday-to-Friday nine-to-five job that's glitz and glam. Not even close. It takes extreme dedication. I've eaten more meals than you can possibly imagine in news cars and live trucks in motion. I've even slept in a live truck on a breaking news story when I had to go live at 11:00 p.m. and wait for the morning crew to relieve me and the photographer at 5:00 a.m. I've covered sickening tragedies like Sandy Hook. That fifteen-hour day was so physically and mentally exhausting. The days following were worse when we had to knock on victims' families' doors. It was heart-wrenching. I've covered so many tragic stories. That was definitely one of the hardest. I think of those families often and even stay in contact with one. This made me realize how valuable family is and just how many holidays and events I've missed out on over the years with my own family. Even though I wasn't physically there, they always found ways to include me and reminded me, "This is your profession, and it requires you to work weird hours and pick up and move often." I think the frequent packing up and moving played a role in my fear of getting too close to people. There were several times it did the opposite when I befriended bad people out of boredom. Shame on me, especially after learning they were not people I should have in my circle.

For every sad or challenging experience throughout this journey, there are also many that make me smile from ear to ear. There are honestly too many to mention. The perks of simply being in the business and getting a press pass for sporting events have always been great. People, for the most part, are intrigued by what you do for a living and want to get to know you. This is always awesome for networking purposes if you're cautious and can realize who's legit and who isn't. I've met so, so many different types of cool and interesting people from celebrities to people living on the streets. I've learned to find unique qualities to admire from so many people I would've never met had I not moved all over the place.

As for exciting stories covered, there are way too many. I already mentioned the World Series and anchoring live from the Major League All-Star Game to even appearing in an HBO documentary and a special on 'ABC's 20/20', "Lost at Sea: The Story of Nathan Carman." It seems to be played quite often. I always get a message from someone, saying, "Hey! I just saw you." I will say though. The stories that make me smile the most are the ones where I was able to truly help people in need—for example, reporting a story about someone who needs a kidney donor ASAP to then turn around and have some stranger contact me and say, "How can I help?" That is the best feeling. I will never forget interviewing a man whose one wish was to speak with Indianapolis Colts player, Hunter Smith. Smith reached out to me and asked for the man's phone number. Smith called him. The man's wife was so thankful this call happened. Her husband died the next day. I'm thankful that being a good journalist has allowed me to be the voice for so many who would otherwise not be heard.

Dad, did anything surprise you about this wild journey? I'm not a parent, so I can't even imagine what it was like having a front-row seat to all of this. Do you have any advice for other parents who have children showing these signs of being an extreme overachiever (or people in general)?

Dad's Comments

Both your mother and I have been working for over forty-five years. I don't believe we could have captured a quarter of the ups and downs, pains and triumphs you expressed here.

You asked if there was anything that surprised me about your journey. Yes, there is. Frankly, I don't understand how you could continue to make the same poor choices over and over again. The choices seem to center on career decisions without fully thinking it through or getting into a relationship that was clearly destined to fail. I can only surmise that there was a voice in your subconscious that overrode simple logic.

I do have two general points I wish to convey to you or anyone else who completes this reading. As a parent, try to convey to your children the importance of balance and a sense of intuition. My wife and I didn't fully accomplish that, or I wouldn't be making these points.

Number 1: A fulfilling life is made up of many things. Examples include career, relationships (family, friends, lovers), health (in general, staying in shape), finance (banking money or barely making ends meet), environment (does your living quarters or the area you live in meet your needs?), and hobbies (what you enjoy doing). There are many other factors. Maslow's hierarchy of needs or various wellness wheels attempt to capture the relative importance of the many factors they offer as being essential to the good life. Each factor is important and necessary in our overall well-being. Different factors predominate various stages of our lives. We can be totally driven by career; a romantic interest; desire to raise children; a zeal to become rich or famous; or a need to chill, relax, and not be pressured in any way. Each factor can, individually, take center stage for a brief time or decades—some for an intense but short time. When all is said and done, it is all about balance. Forfeiting some of one's wellness needs to one overarching activity has consequences. We might soar in our career but crash in our relational interests. Consumed by ambition, our health can suffer mightily. Raising children could stifle our deepest sense of accomplishment. We get a constant pull and tug from all the wellness factors. The key is sorting out which is most important for this moment and which can be delayed but resurrected at a more optimal time. There will be a reckoning as everyone makes choices. Life is a sum total of our choices/decisions. The key is being comfortable with the choices. Don't look back. Don't project into the future.

Number 2: Intuition is sharpened and honed over time by clearly expressing what it is you are feeling and then observing how the gut feeling turned out. You come to understand that your gut decisions get better with a pure heart and clear mind. I think that if you listened more intently to your gut and not your subconscious, better outcomes would have transpired.

Well said, Dad. In the next few chapters (5 through 9), I want to share with you some of the things I've learned that have helped me power through some of my most difficult days along this journey and, most importantly, what I've learned about friendships and relationships. Then, we will circle back with a short recap and my hopes for myself and all of you. ☺

CHAPTER 5

WORK HARD, PLAY HARD, BUT BE PRESENT

My last nineteen years of work experience, coupled with graduate school and college, certainly demonstrates a person who wanted to work hard and get ahead. I would be lying if I said I didn't have any fun throughout the journey. I'm fortunate that I mastered the concept of what it means to work hard, play hard as early as sixteen years old. I can't stress how important it is too for kids to learn how to prioritize. No one becomes a successful, well-rounded person without learning this essential life skill. Dad and Mom, for teaching me this lesson, I thank you.

So how does someone create and maintain a routine that helps them have a productive day? Well, no one can really answer that for you. In my case, doing a good job at work, exercising, eating healthy, making time for phone calls with family and friends, and going out to socialize (one weeknight/one weekend night) is part of my weekly routine. I look at it this way. If I'm working hard during the week, I want to look forward to the weekend by eating something off the "diet" list, having some wine (in moderation 'cause I can't handle hangovers), and maybe spending some money on an affordable outfit, a pedicure, or something to reward myself.

Let's start with diet and exercise. I can't even believe I'm actually writing this right now. I feel like a two hundred-pound weight has been removed from my shoulders. I spent so many days of my life crying, worrying, and wondering how to get my weight under control as I've already discussed. I was afraid what to eat, what not to eat, which diet to follow. At the end of the day, what works for me may not for you. I can't hand you over the diet plan I follow and promise that it will work for you. Some people have specific foods they can and can't eat because of medical conditions. Some people have sixty pounds to lose. Some have five pounds to lose, so the caloric intake, fat intake, carbohydrates, protein, etc. are going to be different. I tried to jump on the low, low, low or no-carb thing, but the body needs carbs—good carbs that are easier to break down. I never quite understood this until I hired a nutritionist. I spent about eight hundred dollars, but it was well worth it because I became educated. At thirty-six years old, I just wanted to build some muscle, not so much suck weight off. I also wanted to feel better, well-nourished, not starved, and not stressed out about what to eat during the day. As a journalist on the go, if you don't pack your meals, you're either not going to eat or your eating snacks from the gas station or fast-food stops. I'm sure that's the case in many professions where you don't have a second to go out and get a real meal.

It's no surprise my day starts off with prepping all my meals, mainly during the workweek. I'm so used to it that it takes me about twenty minutes maximum to cook breakfast, lunch, and dinner, and healthy snacks. This way I know what I'm eating, I'm never sitting there starving, and I'm spiking my metabolism throughout the day. I even have a little food scale and measuring cups that I swear by to make sure I'm eating the right amount of protein and carbs. It does crack me up how small the carb portion of brown rice or sweet potato ends up being; but combined with protein, veggies, and a fat source like extra-virgin olive oil or whole almonds, (measured of course) it's a decent meal.

Once my meals are cooked, I try to hit the gym four to five days a week. I used to go a lot more and try to do an hour-plus of cardio, but that never seemed to work for me. My body never really changed. Once I incorporated some weight training and a really good diet, it all seemed to fall into place. Is my body swimsuit show ready as I write this? No. Would I like to be leaner right now? Yes, but it's the fall season. I'm in the Midwest, and we're in the middle of a pandemic. The only socialization is to meet someone for dinner. The bottom line, the vast majority of people who have those perfectly lean bodies spend time, a lot of time, cooking their meals, avoiding alcohol, and drinking tons of water. I personally feel diet is even more important than exercise. When I worked crazy hours in New York City and was commuting from Connecticut, I went home and went right to bed. I barely exercised for a whole summer, but my diet was on point during my workweek. I cheated a little on the weekends, and I already had a decent physique because of the hard work I put in throughout the years. I could go on and on about this topic, but it comes down to this: take the time to make a healthy diet and exercise part of your routine, part of your lifestyle. You will end up less stressed if you fluctuate a few pounds here and there. Don't go to one extreme of only protein, veggies, water, and extreme exercise to stuffing your face a few days with every gross food you can possibly imagine. If health and fitness is truly a priority, you will work it into your schedule, somehow, someway. No excuses!

Let's talk about trying to incorporate some "play hard" into your routine. This also takes discipline. There's nothing wrong with meeting friends, your significant other, or whoever during your workweek or school week. Again, in moderation. Going out five to seven nights a week, having several drinks, getting minimal sleep, and dragging ass is not the way to have a productive week. I know I can't do it. You feel like crap. Your body craves crap with no sleep and a hangover, and you spend a lot of money. Although if you're a lady, let's face it. A lot of times people send some free drinks your way. Don't drink them if you don't want them. I've also learned to not go out and party like it's New Year's Eve just because you don't have to work the next day. Your days off are supposed to be those where you can break the rules a little bit but also those where you are able to do something productive and not lie around all day long and waste precious time. For example, it's a Sunday, and I'm writing this chapter. Look, I absolutely love fun, laughter, and meeting my friends and family out for dinner. Do it. Enjoy it. Live life, but be responsible. And fit time into your schedule where you can work on your personal goals and hobbies.

There are a few things I wish I could change about my routine over the last few years. One of them—making time to date or at least give decent people a chance. A cup of coffee, a glass of wine, lunch, or dinner is not a big deal. I really kind of wrote dating off because I had it in my mind that until I felt 100 percent sure where I wanted to live for more than a few years at a time, then I should just put potential relationships on the back burner. I've always sort of done this when other relationships failed and ended up going years without dating. I bring this up now because as a woman in her forties who always put career first in her twenties and thirties, I need to at least put myself out there in order to meet someone. Living in the past and fearing another failed relationship or thinking too much in the future is not going to get me anywhere. I'm still a bit guilty for living in the future; and it wasn't until this crazy year of COVID that I said, "I'm DONE living in the past!"

Spirituality has also been nonexistent in my daily routine. So instead of beating myself up, I'm thinking present tense. How can I incorporate this into my daily routine NOW? Well, I was raised Catholic. I went to Catholic school for a few years. My mother's parents are very religious. They pray every day at ninety-three years old. My grandfather had been going to church every Sunday until COVID. I can't even remember the last time I went to church.

I have some dear friends who still go to the Catholic church, and I have some who go to a nondenominational Sunday service. I also have some who have turned to meditation as a form of spirituality. My dad is included in that group. He meditates every single morning and reads books about letting go of those negative voices and "chatter" that we all have, which lead to self-torment. He's tried everything to help me in this important aspect. From mailing me books to sending inspirational quotes via email (he did it every day in South Bend when he knew I was hurting) to buying me audiobooks from top-notch anchors like ABC's Dan Harris's *10% Happier: How I Tamed the Voice in My Head, Reduced Stress without Losing My Edge, and Found Self-Help That Actually Works—A True Story*. I never could find a way to work this into my daily routine. I made excuses about not working this critical self-care component into my life. I'm going to have Dad comment on this chapter and the next one together as they sort of go hand in hand.

CHAPTER 6

═══════════════════════

DISTRACTIONS THAT
DO YOU GOOD

When I originally showed my dad the outline for this book, he was not a fan of the word *distraction*. He was disappointed I was still running from the truth by not making "calming the mind" my main priority. As I said, this will be at the top of my list. I was going to say in the upcoming year, 2021, but why wait? The world is stressful for everyone during a pandemic. Having said that, the point I wanted to make in this chapter is there are certainly ways to add value to your life while down in the dumps instead of turning to drugs, alcohol, overeating, spending, etc.

Physical Fitness

Exercise is also a good distraction when you're sad, depressed, and lonely. I have been on the extreme end of this where it became a distraction that was becoming a main priority. I wanted to do a fitness show. That's when I paid eight hundred dollars for a coach/nutritionist to write a diet and workout plan. I had to check in with him every Saturday and send pictures so he could tweak the diet and exercise plan. I had to drink a gallon and a half of water every day. I was always cooking and preparing meals. I would make up excuses about why I couldn't meet people out for dinner during this time. After about twelve weeks of this, I gave up. I looked pretty lean, but I was miserable. The timing of this type of commitment was way off. My ex-fiancé and I had recently broken up. I started a new job. I was commuting an hour to work at 2:00 a.m., and my sleeping pattern was all over the place. Don't get me wrong. I still think about doing one of these shows, but it needs to be when I have a more flexible work schedule and the timing is right. It's on my bucket list. In the meantime, I'm keeping exercise on my list as a good distraction on a bad day. It doesn't have to be two hours long. A light workout when stressed out is better than no workout.

Hobbies / Side Hustles

Finding a side hustle is also a good distraction that I highly recommend. If you take one look at my social media pages, you will see how obsessed I am with jewelry and dresses. I've always loved shopping and accessorizing. That can get expensive without serious willpower. However, shopping for costume jewelry has always been my guilty pleasure. A boutique owner, Isa, noticed how much I enjoyed this as I became a regular in her store. She said, "You never leave without buying the biggest, boldest earrings or necklace I have displayed." I ended up having many conversations with her about life, relationships, success, failure, and the list goes on. We developed a good rapport. Isa knew something was wrong when I came in one day very quiet and somber. I told her about the breakup with the fiancé. She immediately encouraged me to "find a good distraction," which would be a "no-brainer" in my case.

I replied, "Sell jewelry here or at another store."

I was surprised when she said, "No, curate your own collection. Make it your own jewelry line." I told her the idea sounded awesome, but I had no clue how to make this happen. Isa graciously offered to drive to NYC so we could attend a clothing and accessory wholesale convention at the Javits Center. It was incredible. I felt like a kid at Disney World, overjoyed with all the rides, only this was an endless supply of jewelry. The point of the trip was to show me what the different wholesale price points were and how to mark it up and make a profit.

I wasted no time coming up with the name of my line, "Lure by Logan." I love alliteration, and I needed to find a word that fit the type of statement jewelry I would be selling. *Lure*, by definition, means "the power of attracting or enticing." You will be noticed when wearing Lure by Logan. I always wear solid colors so my jewelry will be the focal point. After the name choice, I got my tax ID, and I was ready to roll. I was thrilled when Isa let me unveil the line in her Branford, Connecticut, boutique. I set up a table as a pop-up vendor. My mom came and helped. It was really a blast. I then did some other pop-ups there during holidays and at a local university. I wouldn't say I made a ton of extra cash. But it was decent, and it was just fun. It made me happy. Isa also let me keep a few items in her store to sell. She was kind enough to only keep less than half of the profit. To this day, I have items in a Westlake, Ohio, boutique where I currently live. I've been slacking with being a pop-up vendor, where you usually make some money within a few hours given the timing and location. The bottom line, Lure by Logan was a good, positive distraction during a difficult time. COVID hasn't helped with in-person sales, but I need to start pushing it on social media.

Lure by Logan launch at Loved Boutique

Learn Something New

If the beginning stages of COVID didn't force you to learn something new out of boredom, it's okay. It's never too late. My boredom started a year earlier. In February 2019 to July 2019, I signed up for a series of online classes at the University of Notre Dame. I earned an executive certificate in nonprofit leadership from the Mendoza College of Business. I was sick of thinking about how I was single, had no life because of my schedule, and was away from my family. It was a lot of work on top of a full-time job, but I worked nights Monday to Friday. There wasn't much to do before my 3:30 p.m. start time besides going to the gym. I figured, *What the heck. I've always had it in the back of my head that if I got out of the TV news business that I may want to do something in the nonprofit industry. I might as well set the potential plan in motion while I have the time.*

Certificate from the University of Notre Dame in nonprofit development

Volunteer / Get Involved

I've always had a passion for nonprofits and causes I believe in, but I never would've predicted earning that certificate. I'm glad I did. I felt a sense of accomplishment. On some of my saddest days and I'm sure many of yours, you've probably been told, "There's someone out there who has it much worse than you do." That's the last thing anyone wants to hear after a devastating breakup, a job loss, or when they feel their world is upside down. If you're not sifting through garbage cans to feed your family or worried about where you will go to sleep at night, then it's a true statement. For this reason, you can't go wrong with volunteering. It's a great way to deflect from your own heartache or issues and help other people who are at rock bottom.

I've been lucky that my job title has been beneficial in organizing charity events and getting a good crowd to attend. Since 2010, I've held toy drives in mid-December. This is usually when there's an indicator of just how many area Salvation Army locations are still in need of toys for families. The idea was sparked when I did a story while living in Providence. My general manager, Steve Doerr, knew that the donations were low that year. He asked if anyone had a personal story, maybe even was a recipient of toy donations in the past. I immediately said, "Yes, my dad. He still remembers the excitement he and his siblings shared when receiving that ONE present from the Salvation Army every year." The thought of that is still heartbreaking for me to even picture. Steve asked if my dad would share this story on television in hopes of tugging at the viewers' heartstrings and getting them to donate. Let's say the story was more successful than anticipated. It started out with pictures of me at about three years old, with tons of presents surrounding me on Christmas Eve, and my dad saying, "You were the only daughter and granddaughter. There was no shortage of presents, love, and attention." Then, it transitioned into my dad's story and how Christmas was a lot different for him as a child. The viewer response was amazing. After the story aired, a local club even agreed to put together a fundraiser in a week's notice to get even more presents donated to Southern New England families.

You don't need to be a news anchor, a politician, or a celebrity to help the less fortunate or those battling deadly diseases. You don't need to be the organizer, and you don't need to be stressed over getting people to attend. Find something that you connect with and will make you feel good about spending your time there. It will make you feel a lot better than sitting at home and crying. In some cases, you may even meet some cool people. Just last year, I simply attended an event for breast cancer awareness and met some great people who I became friends with. We all had a lot in common, and it was a great networking opportunity. It sounds like a win-win to me. You're supporting good causes, meeting potential longtime friends, networking, and not staying home in a funk.

Charity toy drive 2019 in Cleveland with Laura Scott

Step Out of Your Comfort Zone

I never, in a million years, thought that I would enter a pageant. As Dad and I mentioned before, I won Homecoming Queen in high school. It wasn't because I was the "beauty" of the bunch. In fact, the beautiful one, Carolyn, who was the runner-up, should've been the winner, but I think a lot of our classmates voted for me because they noticed how hard I worked at getting into shape and losing weight. Regardless, we were great friends. We got along with everyone, and we both were happy to be nominated. After winning, I received a letter to enter for Miss Massachusetts Homecoming Queen. I had ZERO desire, but I did it because it offered some scholarship / book money for college, and Syracuse was really expensive. Anyway, I entered and won because my speech was great on stage. There was only one other girl. She was beautiful, but it was obvious she had no career aspirations. I ended up winning and representing Massachusetts in the national competition in Anaheim, California. I felt so out of place. However, I've always known how to adapt in any situation. I scanned the room and immediately became friends with the girls who also happened to look out of place. Ironically, they were the girls from Rhode Island, New Hampshire, and Maine. We knew we didn't stand a chance. We still had fun and made the most of the experience. I figured that would be the end of my pageant days at seventeen years old.

I shared that example because I never thought I would enter a pageant ever again. Fast forward to thirty-nine years old. I heard about a New England-based pageant that had to do with charity. In fact, a woman I met in Connecticut won the year before. Your platform on stage is a charity of your choice that you believe in and support. I figured, *Hell, I'm going to come up with my own organization that helps women struggling with self-worth.* That was step 1.

I knew I would be just fine on stage, answering questions, speaking, and looking physically fit in my gown. The thought of parading around in a swimsuit and doing that "walk" was horrifying. However, this was about a year after training for the fitness show I mentioned. I was still in decent shape, and it wasn't like I would be standing in a string bikini where the judges are inspecting every ounce of your body. In this pageant, you were able to wear a sarong, a wrap, even tight fitness clothes if that was what you chose. I always felt fine in a bikini top and skirt because I have a flat stomach and decent legs. The thighs/glutes are STILL a work in progress, but we all (the majority of us) have a problem area.

I mentioned the pageant to my close friend/personal trainer, Tony Salamanca. Without hesitation, he said, "You have to do this. It incorporates fitness, your passion to help women, and you need to get over this perception that your body isn't good enough. You work full-time. You're dedicated to your diet, and you make time for workouts. You will see that your figure is just fine." We both agreed it would be a good opportunity to show the other contestants and the crowd that a well-spoken person, with more than just decent looks, should win a crown and showcase an important mission—REVIVE.

I will say this. I felt confident in my bathing suit, my gown, and speaking on stage. I still felt a bit awkward doing that darn walk that pageant and fitness show contestants do on stage. There was one girl who was really pretty, not really in great physical shape, but she wore a bikini, smiled confidently, and walked that stage like a pro. I was impressed. I also witnessed firsthand that everybody has something attractive about them. The most gorgeous one may be the most awkward when it comes to speaking.

At the end of the day, a woman who was always, always so self-critical about her body based on the "chubby childhood trauma" stepped out of her comfort zone. I'm glad I did it. I realized my body is not nearly as bad as I imagine it in my mind. I'm well-spoken, and most importantly, "I AM REAL!" What you see is what you get. I can't tell you how many of these women told me that day and in the following days that they enjoyed being around me and respected my ability to speak well and from the heart. I think the judges noticed this as well. I made eye contact with every one of them. Anyone who speaks in front of people regularly knows how important this is. They loved my concept of REVIVE, and I won a crown. I did not win first place, which was Miss New England States, but I did win Miss Connecticut New England States. More on REVIVE next, but first…

Dad, what do you think of these examples of good distractions, most importantly my hesitation and your frustration on how I couldn't seem to work in some type of calming the mind? How has it helped you, a person who also likes to follow a routine and keep busy?

Workout session with trainer Tony Salamanca

Pageant photos

Dad's Comments

First, I'm proud of the woman you have created and your many accomplishments. Impressive. Each and every accomplishment was squarely on you. You focused in on areas you felt needed improvement (nutrition and working out), stepped out of your comfort zone by entering beauty pageants, continued your education, and worked to better the community by selflessly volunteering. I wish we all could say we are striving as hard as you to better ourselves and the world.

As you let the readers know at the start of this chapter, I'm a little disappointed you continually needed to find distractions. What are we being distracted from? Why do we need to be distracted? Without distractions, we are left with dealing with who and what we are. One has to be comfortable living in one's own skin. One has to be compassionate toward one's own self. No one is perfect. I mean no one, but we try to do our best. We succeed and fail. At the end of the day, all alone, we have to like ourselves. If we don't, how can anyone else? Why would anyone else be attracted to a miserable human being?

My frustration is that I had been trying (and not succeeding) in getting you to try an alternative path other than listening to the chatter in your mind about the miserable past and the catastrophic future. The associated visual scenarios your mind creates only amplifies the debilitating stress you succumb to. You are unable to have a clear mind and make good decisions about the present. Your journey has been winding, and you don't know why. My guess is some of your actions would have been different had they been informed by a clear mind rather than the sum of your fears. It is a wonderful feeling to make a decision and be fully comfortable with it and not constantly second-guess yourself. You, no one else, have made the right decision for the right reasons. You have dealt with your subconscious mind and overcame its false narratives.

Meditation is a way of life. You have to put yourself in a place, an environment that is quiet and comfortable. It's so important to your being that you make time for it gladly. You welcome giving up some other activity to partake in it. You listen to all the monkey chatter and see all the cinematic visions your mind creates and just observe without analyzing or getting attached to them. These vanish. And miraculously, life's pressing issues are laid out clearly in a path. The steps necessary to accomplish your goals or understand what is really in your heart are obvious. Over time, with increasing mindfulness, you rarely get stressed. You see the issues and know what is important. You make good decisions. If things don't work out, you know you did the best you could and it wasn't meant to be. Wanting something and that something being the best for you aren't always compatible. Let it go. The true best thing will reveal itself to you after further pondering. It cannot be forced.

Meditation and mindfulness did not come to me spontaneously. You have to be at a place in your life where you do want to be at peace with yourself, and you work at it. It is not easy. It takes a lot of time and effort. However, given your string of accomplishments, it is clearly within your reach.

CHAPTER 7

REVIVE
ARE YOU REALLY READY TO BE REVIVED?

REVIVE was first presented on stage at the Miss New England States pageant in November 2017. Here is the breakdown: R, respect and love yourself; E, end the cycle of unhealthy relationships; V, vent to others; I, identify your unique strengths; V, verify problem behaviors; E, express emotions effectively.

For years, I googled "self-esteem/self-worth workshops." I never ever had great luck with one-on-one therapy. As an adult in my late thirties (2017), I knew I wasn't alone in this self-destructive path of trying to always be prettier, thinner, building a better résumé, and always working myself to death. I wanted to meet these women, hear their stories, and share with them. I just never seemed to find anything like REVIVE, which is why I came up with this concept. I didn't really love myself. R—I seemed to be involved in unhealthy relationships. E—I found it helpful venting to women in similar situations. V—I had come across so many women who sold themselves short; for example, marrying young and never getting a job, losing themselves, feeling like they were a housewife from the 1940s with no purpose other than taking care of the kids, the husband, and keeping the house clean. No hobbies, no talents, no personal, professional goals or accomplishments. They needed serious assistance in discovering their unique strengths—I.

The next V (verify problem behaviors and addictions) is a bit complicated. We all have some type of character flaw that we're not proud of and hate to admit. In my case, I had a pattern of using text messaging as an alternative to just fire off any horrible thoughts or feelings going through my mind. If someone said something mean, I would find a way to fire back something worse. I know many have been guilty of this. In my case, it was becoming very problematic to the point I was spending half my days feeling guilt and having to give a proper apology. I don't know why for years and years I just couldn't shake this absurd pattern of behavior. I know others have told me when people were mean to them or "wronged" them, they would do other things like sulk, overeat, drugs, get drunk all the time, damage the person's property, and the list goes on. Truthfully, using text messages to say stupid, childish, mean things to people was my outlet. It has accounted for 98 percent of the most embarrassing things I've done. Messages sent when pissed off or angry don't go away. You look like a complete idiot. I'm relieved to say that I do NOT do that anymore. I have a male friend who's a few years older than me who does this from time to time when irritated or not hearing what he wants. When he does, I pick up the phone and leave a voice mail (if he doesn't answer), telling him to call me back. An argument or potential argument should be between you and the other person, not for you to show others and them to show others. I would say this sums up the last two bullet points of REVIVE. V, verify problem behaviors; and E, express emotions effectively. Many people struggle in their own ways to express how they're feeling from friendships, relationships, family members, and bosses. There is a way to do this, but some need more practice than others.

Failed Forms of Therapy

Now that you know the "who" and "what" my reasons are for creating REVIVE, you're probably wondering when, where, and how I came up with this program. After spending the first few years post-

South Bend "reporting facts and running from the truth," I knew I needed therapy. Even with my career back on a great path anchoring, reporting, being on the investigative team, and teaching at local colleges, I still felt like a zero. I was in a relationship where neither one of us were happy, yet no one would cut the cord. Crying in the bathroom at work and barely able to get out of bed in the morning were becoming a regular thing.

Between 2014 and 2016, I went to three different therapists. The first two were women. One of them was hilarious, energetic, and you could tell loved her job. I bet she would be phenomenal at helping kids, teens, and adults who lacked motivation, were hooked on drugs, or had anger issues. I don't think she was a good person to give advice on bad relationships. I actually feel like we could've been friends. She was great, just not a good fit for my situation. Sidebar: I even gave her another shot in 2017 when I was working in New York City. She advised me to give a very handsome, charismatic, wealthy guy a second chance because she thought he truly liked me based on his text messages I showed her. Oh, did I mention he was a cocaine addict? That was the day I decided to politely part ways again. I've never done cocaine and never will.

Next on the list in the 2014–2015 time frame was a woman who literally made me want to fall asleep every time I walked in her home office. She was dull and seemed so looped out on antidepressants. For some reason, all she wanted to do was talk to me about the news. She wanted to know about my colleagues at the station! So much for therapy. That was a TOTAL waste of time.

This brings us to 2016. I moved on to a new station in Connecticut. My ex-fiancé and I parted ways. I was commuting an hour to work and nearly seventy-five minutes home in traffic. I felt lost and confused. I wanted to find a different type of therapy rather than talk therapy. I had heard a lot about cognitive behavioral therapy. It helps to let go of negative thoughts and emotions that may be clouding your way of thinking and controlling the way you react to certain situations. It's very interactive, and I feel it holds you more accountable in breaking bad patterns. The therapist was a man. At first, I thought, *Wow. This may be just what I need.* It didn't take very long for him to start asking about the news business. He seemed a little too impressed that I was on the news and was one of his patients. I recall him even asking me to find a way to get his business on the air by doing some type of story encouraging people to seek this type of therapy. I let it go for a few sessions but ended up walking away feeling frustrated, annoyed, and that I would need to accept living my life sad, alone, and being a workaholic to get through each day.

After a month or so of no therapy, I didn't want to give up on myself. I knew I wasn't suicidal or needing to be hospitalized. However, I truly wanted a period of days in a row spent completely on me and getting me to feel worthy, like myself a little bit more, and learn to heal from past relationships. I knew I only had two weeks of vacation to last me an entire year. I was fortunate to have a boss who had a heart and actually cared about his employees. I told him what was going on and asked if I could use my vacation time all at once and go to a group therapy program at a hospital an hour away close to my parents. It was four days a week from 9:00 a.m. to 1:00 p.m. Without hesitation, he said, "Erin, it's no problem. It's nobody's business. I've been a manager for a long time. You're not the first and won't be the last employee to come to me with a similar request." I immediately thanked him and made the arrangements.

The first day of this experience was a bit strange. Everyone introduced themselves by first name and shared why they were there. This was a group of ten including men and women. I would say the age range was low twenties to fifty. Some were dealing with depression, drug or alcohol addiction, and difficulties dealing with loss whether it be death or traumatic breakups. Once it was my turn to explain why I was there, you could tell people were surprised due to my accomplishments and job as a news anchor.

There was one young guy in particular who I remember. His name was Keith. He pulled me aside and said something like, "Hey, you shouldn't be so hard on yourself. You have a good job, and it sounds like you have a good family. Everything will be okay." The next day, Keith showed up with a number of index cards in his hand. You could see they weren't blank. During the short break, he handed them to me. They all had different quotes written on them. There were nearly a dozen pertaining to loving yourself and forgiving yourself. He said he wanted me to read them every day. The quotes helped him out after a bad breakup and when he was really doubting himself. More than four years later, I still have them. One is titled, "Being Lovable." It reads, "I will tell myself that I'm lovable. Just because some people haven't been able to love me in ways that worked doesn't mean that I'm unlovable. I've had lessons to learn, and some of them hurt deeply. But I can still love and be loved." Another one was titled, "Rescuing Myself." It reads, "I will not wait around for someone to come to my aid and rescue me. Tell yourself that you are not helpless. Although maybe help may come, realize and believe that you're your own rescuer. Your relationships will start to dramatically improve when you stop rescuing others and stop expecting others to rescue you." How great are the quotes? I thought it was so incredibly nice that he took the time to write these and share them.

Another thing I remember was a bit of advice given from a guy in his thirties who had battled drug addiction for years and was several months sober. He said he noticed his pattern of drug use when he was worrying about certain things he created in his mind. Looking back, they were things he really didn't need to worry about. He advised us all to make a list of any worry that crossed our minds throughout each day. At the end of the week, we were to go back and highlight any of the things that we really had reason to worry about. We all found there were very few, if any, to be highlighted.

At the end of the two weeks, I felt better and realized I didn't have things as bad as I thought I did. Still, it didn't matter. I went back to putting way too much pressure on myself in every aspect of my life. I chose to once again "report facts and run from the truth." I remember saying to myself, "Forget dating. Forget going out. I need to feel better, look better, and be more successful." So I made sure my schedule was jam-packed by going to the gym, networking with others in the industry via email or social media, updating my résumé reel, or anything BUT focusing on the REAL issue here—I WASN'T HAPPY. I thought maybe if I worked in NYC on television with some of the most talented journalists in the industry that I would prove the haters wrong, feel better about myself, and everything would fall into place. That was not the case at all. I told you I was spending nearly four hours or more each shift commuting. I was constantly exhausted and never had time for anything.

Fourteen months had passed since the group therapy experience I described. I felt even more depressed. I had just turned thirty-nine years old. My younger brother was engaged, and I still found myself attracted to people who were bad boys with issues. It's ridiculous because at the end of the day, I knew I would NEVER end up with this type of guy, let alone introduce them to my parents! Why on earth was I tormenting myself? I needed to know, so I tried again.

Almost Time for Erin to BE Revived?

I was able to find an all-women's group therapy program close to where I lived and did not interfere with my work schedule. I can honestly say this is the "when," "where," and "how" of REVIVE's creation. I loved that this was a group of all women. It was easier to share stories and talk about what we were truly feeling at the time. We did an exercise where we had to describe how we think people view us versus how we feel inside. On the outside, I wrote "made-up, perfect hair, full of energy, perfect outfit, chatty, exuding confidence, and knowledgeable in all subject matters." On the inside, I wrote "bored, lonely, scared, sad, angry, burned out, anxious, going through the motions, somewhat hopeless, and embarrassed I'm not married with kids." I often look at this two-sided mask-shaped piece of paper and shake my head. It makes me sad to think I was feeling that way for so long.

This program included about ten sessions. After about three, I called one of my really good guy friends, Charlie. I explained that I liked the concept of what we were doing and how I envisioned a program for women in a non-stereotypical setting, one not affiliated with a hospital. Again, after years of googling "self-esteem workshops for women," I truly couldn't find anything. There are soooo many women who go through ups and downs in life and don't believe in themselves. They could use a good REVIVE session even if it's simply to "vent" to other women. Charlie has created programs of his own pertaining to men and women who've been incarcerated and are transitioning back into the workforce and those who've later gone above and beyond. He encouraged me to take notes, come up with my own program, and start out as a community organization and, possibly down the road, a 501(c)(3).

A week or so later, I explained all the bullet points of REVIVE to Charlie. He loved it, still loves it. This was in September or October 2017. As I mentioned, I presented REVIVE on stage at the charity pageant in November 2017. I was still working in New York City, so it was difficult to get the first workshop series put together. I had to find someone to donate the space and of course find the women who wanted to sign up. In April 2018, it happened. I allowed eight women to attend the three-session workshop series in New Haven, Connecticut. The whole point was to have an intimate, comfortable setting, so I didn't want more than eight. This was a free program for women. Supplies were needed, and food would be provided. My friends, family, and area businesses helped me put on a spring fashion show fundraiser to cover those costs. I'm still grateful how well this was received by everyone!

One of the sessions included a lesson with Wendy Perrotti, a well-established life coach from Connecticut. We have a history of working together. I'm not easily impressed with people, but she impressed me off the bat when I first met her in 2015. I wanted her to teach these women about the way the brain works and why we often times become our own worst enemy. She also talked about effective coping skills when you feel yourself start to spiral out of control. I think the women truly enjoyed the program overall. One of the participants in her late thirties or early forties said, "My thoughts on REVIVE are that it gets participants to hone in on themselves, helps them to become aware of unconscious parts of themselves, and helps them to move forward in a confident, empowered way" (E. A.). The plan was to hold another three-week series in September 2018 once summer winded down. I ended up moving to Cleveland and put it on the back burner.

More Than Ready to BE Revived / Almost Revived According to Wendy

In June 2020, once we all became accustomed to this COVID world, I wanted to bring the program back in the worst way. Once businesses started opening up, a Cleveland area gym donated space, and one of my close friends offered to sponsor the event through his real estate business. This time, I wanted the program to be for teen girls because that's where the self-doubt really starts. It certainly did in my case. My boss allowed me to mention on air that the event would be held in late August 2020. I got a huge response. I felt bad I could only take the first eight who reserved a spot. It was a little different due to COVID restrictions, but we made it work. Wendy even joined us virtually.

It's interesting because as much as I loved/love the REVIVE program, there were times where I couldn't stand it. Why? It's because I still couldn't understand why I didn't fully love and appreciate myself. When I first hired Wendy as my own personal life coach in 2015, I was wasting her time and somewhat mine. Frequent comments coming from me were "I will never meet a nice guy who truly likes me for me," "I guess I'm just meant to spend all my time working myself to death to prove all the haters wrong," and "If I'm on the news and I can't find a good guy, then who on earth would want me?" My thought process got slightly better over time as we worked together, but those comments weren't erased even in 2018. We never lost touch when I moved to Cleveland, but I hired her to work with me again in May 2020. This COVID way of life was really, really starting to get to me. I told her I liked my job as the 5:00/5:30/7:30 p.m. anchor, but I was lonely. I really missed my family, and I refused to do the online dating thing. Let's face it. There's really not an easy way to meet new people in person during a pandemic. Mingling at bars, restaurants, and stadiums is not allowed. She told me she heard something different from me, perhaps a different tone. This time it was an Erin who finally realized she doesn't need a man, a boss, or any person to dictate her opinion of herself—an Erin who knew her life wasn't exactly where she wanted it to be but an Erin who was on a real path to finding true happiness. No settling, reasonable expectations, and having people in her life with similar core values.

It's pretty clear therapy never worked for me. I truly believe no matter what outlet any of us choose, we have to be READY and willing to be HELD ACCOUNTABLE. It's liberating to finally say that no other person is in charge of my happiness. I am. If somebody doesn't think I'm pretty enough, smart enough, or good enough, then so be it.

I'm still working on building a well-rounded life including friends; family; possibly a great guy in my life, who has the same values, and fulfilling additional career aspirations. This includes being a motivational speaker, writing another book, and building REVIVE.

I asked Wendy Perrotti to say a few words about how she feels life coaching clicked for me and how it could possibly work for you or someone you know who just kept going around and around in circles with no real changes. Here's what she had to say:

> I'm guessing if you've read this far, you can relate to some of what Erin has experienced. The truth is, all of those feelings and struggles are a natural part of being human. Here's what's going on. We all have that voice in our heads that tells us that we're not good enough. Depending on the things you've personally experienced, that voice may say things like "you're too fat, "too loud," "too small," "too stupid," or even, "unworthy," that voice is simply you, protecting yourself from anything you perceive as harmful. If someone made you feel ugly, you're likely to have created a voice that tells you not to do things that you fear may expose you to that kind of ridicule again.
>
> If you had a hard time in school and felt embarrassed or ashamed about not having the answer, that voice in your head is going to call

you stupid every time you're about to speak up in an effort to protect you from further humiliation.

Believe it or not, that nasty little voice has been your life-long BFF, protecting you from everything that you fear. At some point however, we all recognize that our little voice has over-served its purpose and is only holding us back from the things we really want most. This is where Erin was when I met her. She knew that she no longer wanted to fight with herself. Intellectually, she got that there was nothing wrong with her. That if other people had happy relationships, she could too. And so, she tried to fix it. Of course, it didn't really work.

Erin's not alone. This is where most people get stuck. We think that "doing" is enough to make things happen because it usually does. Want a clean floor? Get a broom and sweep. In order to make anything happen, intentional action *is* required. The problem is that it doesn't work when the thing you want to do is in association with the voice in your head. Here's why. After years and years of telling yourself that you're not good enough for something, you come to BELIEVE it. And belief is the thing that underpins the ultimate success or failure of everything you set out to do.

Believe that you can, and each time you try and fail, you'll learn and grow until you create or achieve what you're working towards. BUT, if underneath it all you believe that you can't—that it's not for you, each time you try and fail you're strengthening the belief that you can't. And the more the evidence you can't do it or have it builds up, the more you fall into old, defensive and protective behaviors that make success all but impossible. You stay stuck, trying harder and harder while continuing to get the same result. This is why Erin felt like she was "wasting her time and mine" in 2015. She so desperately wanted to move on that she kept trying—taking action—before her belief about who she is and what is possible for her had a chance to begin to shift.

Growth is rarely a linear process and Erin's experience is not an uncommon one. Without an opportunity to have someone reflect long-held limiting beliefs back at us, we have a difficult time making the types of behavioral shifts required to make all of that "trying" payoff.

Flash forward. Erin hadn't actually been wasting time in 2015. Slowly but surely, the concepts we worked on began to sink in. While Erin continued to work on the REVIVE program, pursue her career etc., below the radar she was testing her environment against a fledgling set of new beliefs. And over time (even though she was somewhat unaware of it) her belief system started to shift. So, when we picked up coaching in May 2020, the woman that came to our sessions had grown. *This* Erin BELIEVED in the possibility that she could have a life filled with meaningful work, loving relationships, and contentment. She was also less attached to that life having to look one particular way. This paves the way for opportunity and new outcomes. This is where magic begins to happen.

REVIVE logo

Picture of first
REVIVE workshop

REVIVE fashion show

CHAPTER 8

RELATIONSHIPS

At forty-two years old, twice engaged, and currently single, I am certainly not a relationship expert. However, some of the lessons I've learned firsthand are very valuable. I can't even begin to count the number of times I've cringed when hearing "timing is everything" and "it will happen when you least expect it." I hate to say it. There's a lot of truth to these statements. You can't force someone to be ready when you are, and you really can't go out there searching for love or trying to MOLD people into the person YOU want them to be.

Timing

I mentioned I was first engaged at twenty-two years old. I had just turned twenty-two. It was five months after graduating from college. This was my first love. I never really had a serious boyfriend in high school. I didn't really have any experience with a relationship. My ex-fiancé, who was one year older, had at least two really serious girlfriends before me and both lasted a few years. He was leaps and bounds more mature than me. After I graduated, we were living together in Providence. He had a full-time job, and I was commuting back and forth from Boston to graduate school. I was dying to be engaged to him because we were living together. I felt I was sacrificing a lot by living just steps from where he worked and nowhere close to where I would be spending ten hours a day five days a week. I got what I wanted. He proposed. I was so happy, but deep down, I was terrified. I remember thinking, *How the heck am I going to pursue my career if I get married this young? He has huge career aspirations, and so do I.* I would cause stupid, ridiculous arguments to sabotage the relationship. Here's a great guy with good values, morals, and intelligence. The bottom line, the timing was way off. I was immature and far from ready to be a wife and have kids in my midtwenties.

Surprisingly, when I hit my late twenties and early thirties, I was not in the "I NEED TO GET MARRIED NOW" mode as most of my friends were. I was still putting my career first as were my two college best friends. Once I turned thirty-three and was the maid of honor in both of their weddings, that's when I started to get a little concerned. I was engaged again at thirty-six years old. It just wasn't going to work. He had already been married and had two kids. I knew deep down he really didn't want more. At that time, I really did. We didn't even live in the same state. I didn't want to move. He didn't want to move, and the situation just wasn't going to work. There were too many things I wanted that I wasn't getting out of this relationship, and I'm sure he could say the same.

There's No Such Thing as Fixing Someone

Let's bring back the quote my friend Keith shared with me in group therapy. "I will not wait around for someone to come to my aid and rescue me. Tell yourself that you are not helpless. Although maybe help may come, realize and believe that you're your own rescuer. Your relationships will start to dramatically improve when you stop rescuing others and stop expecting others to rescue you." It is so true. The purpose of a relationship is not to serve as the other person's mother, father, or rescuer. Two people in a relationship should complement each other, be a team, and bring out the best in each other.

If you think you can "fix" a person or mold them into the person you want them to be, think again. It is NOT going to happen, especially if the person is past a certain age. People become set in their ways. If I could combine the qualities of two of the men I fell for in life, I would have the perfect person. Does that even exist? My point is, you can't force someone to text you multiple times a day or not text you multiple times a day, be a little more jealous or not jealous at all. It's always been important to me that my boyfriend appreciates that I work hard, and I prefer one who works just as hard. I've never really clicked with lazy. However, I can't order a grown man how to structure their day. I also find a man who really values his family attractive. Even if they have/had kids from a previous marriage, I would still expect him to make the kids a priority before me. Kids deserve family time. Some of my friends are constantly fighting with their men because the kids come first. See, we are all different. Everyone has certain things that make them tick, that make them happy. If you communicate these wants and needs early in the relationship and both parties aren't delivering, there's no sense tormenting yourself or the other person when it's not working. I'm not sure why it took me so many years to master the concept of walking away when relationships made me cry more than smile.

Remember I mentioned in the last chapter how many times I've embarrassed myself by texting mean things? I know for certain I'm not the only who's done this many times during a breakup. If you factor in texting while drinking wine! That can be a total evil nightmare. This picture you see here with all these old phones, including a Blackberry (always loved the Blackberry, lol) account for so many of my embarrassing moments. In fact, one of my ex-boyfriends said to me many times, "Stop letting these 'machines' ruin everything I love about you." We even did a little experiment where we blocked each other from text and could only call. We got along a lot better, but c'mon, that's ridiculous. We all need a little self-control and not impulsively hit the send button. Save yourself the embarrassment, PLEASE! When you're in the midst of a breakup or any heated argument, don't text mean things. The next day, you want to crawl in a cave because of what you wrote, and you feel terrible. I still remember some of the mean things men have said to me over text and things I've said to them. Even after an apology, I truly feel words hurt very deeply.

The "MACHINES" that got me in trouble

A Mutual Give-and-Take

I truly believe there needs to be an equal give-and-take, or at least sixty-forty. I've been guilty of giving too much and also taking too much. I don't know about you; but a man who is constantly doing the calling, texting, buying me gifts, and smothering me is a total turn off. Some of my friends feel the opposite. They want a guy who makes them the center of their universe. I think that is boring and unfair to the other person. I've had people say to me over and over and over again, "You need to marry a man with money to take care of you." Of course, it would be nice to have someone financially well-off, but I too want to be a strong contributor to our finances. I mean, if I were at home raising kids close in age, then by all means I would be blessed that I could take some extra time off or have a lighter work schedule. I think it's important though to have your own identity as a spouse, even if it's a part-time job doing something you enjoy.

I grew up in a home where I noticed a lot of give-and-take. My dad did all the yard work. My mom did all the laundry, cooking, and cleaning. There are also many times where they cooked and cleaned together. They are a team. They take care of each other. My mom will pack him a lunch. He will wipe the snow off the car for her. It's the little things that matter. There is not one sole person kissing the other person's ass. He keeps her in check when she does annoying things, and he does the same. They are great together, but they are two people that are grounded enough to stand on their own two feet.

Don't Compare Your Love Story to Others'

I swear a lot of times I feel my parents' love story has helped me immensely and hurt me immensely. Here's the deal. NO ONE'S HAPPILY-EVER-AFTER STORY IS THE SAME! My dad and I both told you in the beginning of this book they both came from two ENTIRELY different backgrounds. I mean polar opposites! She had already started her career as a teacher when they first met. He had already gone to several different colleges and hadn't yet graduated. When things started to get serious, he got serious. He left town, went to get his college degree, and hoped to God when he was done doing what he felt he needed to be a good partner that she would be single. Back then there were no cell phones, emails—nothing but good old landlines. The best part of this love story is him knocking on my great-grandmother Maria's door. She had a winter home in Miami. That's where my dad was going to college. He told her he needed money to fly home and surprise my mom. He was willing to paint for her or do some odd jobs around the house. Little did he know that would mean painting nearly every room. Guess what? He ended up enjoying many meals and feeling so much love from a family. Fast-forward, he graduated, proposed, and they celebrated forty-four years of marriage in September 2020. He has no problem at all admitting he wanted to change when he met my beautiful, thoughtful, amazing mother. HOWEVER, he told me time and time again he was in his early to midtwenties when there's still room to change your ways. He was watching me try and do this with men who were in their forties. At that point, it's a little too late. A man at that age has likely already been married and is set in his ways. I didn't listen to him or any therapist or Wendy when they repeatedly told me that same thing. Instead, I would believe the opposite and repeatedly tell myself, "If I was worth it, he would make some changes for me. If I was pretty enough, he would never want to lose me. If I was successful enough, he would never want to lose me." If I lost that idea that "changing for someone is the true definition of love," I would've saved myself so, so, so much heartache.

Do Not Chase, Do Not Be Desperate, but Do Not Give Up

If I can teach women (and men) one thing and one thing only, it's this. Do NOT base your self-worth on whether or not someone wants you. It's pathetic. There have been MANY good, quality, handsome, kind men who've wanted me, but for whatever reason, I wasn't interested due to unresolved feelings for others or just simply—here we go—BAD TIMING. It doesn't mean that person wasn't worthy of me. Think about how stupid that sounds. Look, if someone doesn't want to date you, it's their loss. Now, if someone doesn't want to date you because you lie, cheat, drink too much, and have addiction problems or vice versa, that's a different story. If you want that person in your life, you work together and try to make things right. After too many failed attempts, then it's time to walk away. You're in charge of deciding how many is too many. Not the other person, YOU. When you or the other person decide it's over, let it go. Is it hard? In many cases, absolutely. In others, not so much. Good riddance. However, when you start blowing up someone's phone, begging them to be with you, you look completely ridiculous. You've just lost your self-respect. You ended up grieving two losses, them and you.

Dad, you've been married forty-four-plus years, and you and Mom, in my opinion, seem like equals. No one person is wearing the pants in this relationship. So what's the secret to true love and happiness in a relationship?

Dad's Comments

A true relationship doesn't just abruptly end. It has a beginning, a middle, and an end. You see, it's the middle that is important. All beginning relationships are a wonder, a joy. It's the middle that dictates how it will all end. Your partner quietly (or not so quietly) sends constant signals to you about how the relationship is going for them. Are they starting to argue more, be unreasonable, lie, be late, be apathetic about what to do or not to do, want to hang out with their friends with more frequency and duration, or cheat? These are more clear indicators that there needs to be more communication, better understandings, less selfishness, and respect. No relationship is without its ups and downs, highs and lows. It's how the two individuals handle the good and the bad. There are no surprises. It's just that one person wasn't listening, seeing, or comprehending what was directly in front of them.

A long-term relationship is really a partnership. One can't or shouldn't go into a relationship thinking the other party will take care of all their needs. Guess what? The other party has needs too. There is something about you that the other party finds worthy of their love and commitment. Each shares the household work, child-rearing, financial stability, joy, and pain. Nothing in life is fifty-fifty. Sometimes you are pulling more than your share of the load, and at other times, your partner is. If one is aware of their partner's frame of mind, they can see and sense what is important in the moment and react appropriately.

Life has its ups and downs. No one can escape what confronts us. It is important to fully embrace the joys that come along and, alternatively, to work together through the hard times. We learn that, together, we can overcome the hardships. Those who have resilience mellow with age gracefully. With time, love becomes shared affection and respect.

CHAPTER 9

FRIENDSHIPS

When I think of the word *friend*, I feel a sense of happiness. Over the last ten years, I've hit the jackpot in this category. I was able to decipher who my true friends, my acquaintances (or slightly more), and the users (or fair-weather friend) are. My attitude is "the more the merrier." It's allowed me to meet some great people and also those who I'm sure took pleasure in seeing me fail.

I know not many can call one or both their parents their best friends. I'm honored and blessed to say that I can. I know I've mentioned my college friends, Deb and Jenn, several times. Yes, they are my best friends too. However, all of us agree there's something amazing about having our parents on that list. Once Deb lost her mother, it became even more clear how fortunate I am to have BOTH parents to pick up the phone and call at any hour. They don't judge. They love you unconditionally, yet they call you out when necessary in ways that maybe a bestie might not. Although, Jenn and Deb keep it real with me as I do with them! The bottom line, on my absolute worst day, I have four people who I know I can count on for anything. I know everyone's family dynamics are different and it's just not in the cards to call a parent or even a sibling a best friend. If it's possible to repair any of your relationships with immediate family, I highly recommend it. Life is too short.

With Jenn and Deb, I have a twenty-year-plus friendship that has been consistent. Some of the ugliest fights I've had have been with them. They've said some horrible things to me, and I have done the same with them. Just this morning, I was laughing with Jenn about a fight we got into in 2009. I flew from South Bend to Syracuse to go to a Syracuse-Notre Dame basketball game that started at noon. I was thirty-one years old, and Jenn was thirty-three. Let's just say we acted like we were sixteen. We were trashed when her dad and mom picked us up from the game to go to dinner. We looked like idiots. In the car, we argued about something stupid. I decided to sit in the car and not go into the restaurant. Ten minutes later, Jenn came out laughing and saying we were both being ridiculous. I started laughing as well, and the night went on with a lot of water and carbs to get rid of the buzz. Hey, we weren't driving, and the game was at noon. However, we both agree way too many stupid, pathetic arguments stem from too many drinks. Know your limit and know what topics to avoid in these situations.

A True Friend Isn't Jealous

I consider these two women my sisters. I would trust them with anything. I know they feel the same about me. God forbid I were stranded with one of their husbands, or them with one of my boyfriends or exes I was in love with, none of us would worry for a second that something inappropriate would be said or done. I hate to say it, but I know we all know this. Many women are jealous of their best friends. I see it every day. I think to myself, *How is that really your friend?* Jenn is constantly complimenting me on my green eyes and staying in shape. I'm constantly complimenting her on her stunningly gorgeous hair and impeccable makeup. I'm proud of her for being extremely successful in her career and as a mother. She's proud of me for pursuing my career that I wanted since she met me at eighteen years old. She's also proud of me for packing up and moving more than a dozen times and adapting to my surroundings even in some not-so-ideal situations. Then, there's Deb. She's a doctor—an ob-gyn delivering babies all the time! She wasn't brought up with money. She was always the one who had a job in college to make ends meet and still did well in school. Her hard work certainly paid off.

She's an amazing mother and so giving to everyone in her presence. She's often said to me, "I've always wanted to be like you. On the news, perks everywhere, a lot of attention, etc." The lesson here is a true friend is never jealous of the other person. You are proud of them and happy for them. Does it bother me that I don't have a beautiful house and children like Deb and Jenn? Sure. However, I've never, for one second, been jealous. Our lives and career paths were completely different. I know someday they will both be my maids of honor. I've already asked them twice before! Lol. Ladies, you may be nearing fifty years old by time you stand up for me! I'm not in a rush like I was in my thirties!

Friendships Change

I always had a lot of friends throughout childhood and high school. It's funny because during my first engagement at twenty-two, so many were on the list to be in the wedding or at least be invited. That list got smaller when I was engaged at thirty-six. Now, there's really only one guy from high school and one woman, Dali, who ever dials or texts my number. I really didn't even hang out with Dali much in high school. We reconnected in our early thirties and have been communicating ever since. I believe we hit it off due to the many similarities at that point in our lives. She moved away, went to college, and pursued her career in fashion designing and later, real estate. She, too, wasn't and still isn't married with children. We were raised in a town where few people have left. They met their spouses there and settled down. They're all doing well and have raised nice children. I knew all along, deep down that would never be my thing: to stay put in my hometown. I wanted to explore, meet new people—see new things. However, there are some people I truly wish I had stayed in better contact with, but life happens. In that case, sending an out-of-the-blue message to them has always made me feel good. I know they, too, liked receiving the message and reminiscing about old times. In fact, I'm thinking of Kim June from high school right now and Rachelle and Laura from college. I know I could meet up with them, and it would be just like old times.

Jennifer DeStefano-Stagnitti and me

Dr. Deb Prinz-Gentile and me

A True Friend Is Forgiving

When people are hurting, feeling physically ill, or just lost in life, they may act out of character and say and do things they regret. As they say, "Misery loves company." In early 2016, Dali and I were both not in a happy place. It was great to have someone to share those concerns with, ask for advice, and not have to bother your other friends who have children. I went to visit her a few months after a previous visit. I was expecting to have a great time once again. She didn't feel well. I was annoying her by trying to squeeze in gym visits and meal prep, and it just got bad. She said some horrible things, and I fired back. I didn't know what the heck was going on, but I stopped replying because I knew it was getting ugly. I also knew that someday down the road, we would end up speaking again. Months later, I checked my Facebook messages. There was a very long apologetic message, explaining what she was dealing with at that time. I wrote back and told her not to sweat it. We've all done and said things during times where we're not feeling ourselves and dealing with life's constant curveballs. A friend forgives and forgets. Unless a dear friend has cheated with your man, kept an ugly secret, or done something horrible, accept their apology. I've been on the other end doing the apologizing and putting myself out there. It's absolutely necessary if the friendship means something to you.

A True Friend Genuinely Feels Sad When You're Hurting

I could write a novel when it comes to this topic. That awful day in South Bend and the days that followed taught me a valuable lesson. The people who picked up the phone to ask if I was okay actually cared. They didn't wait to send me a phony social media message. As awkward as it was for them, they called.

I will never forget walking into the woman's home where I was living and renting a room. She was at the kitchen table, reading the police report to one of her male friends. As if it weren't colorful enough in all of the local newspapers, she went out of her way to go to the police department to get it printed out. I was already so beside myself with all the public humiliation, then to go home and see this? This hurtful moment was immediately followed by kindness. I called my friends, Jack and Christa, a married couple with two boys. I asked if I could come by and talk. When I got out of my car, they saw me sobbing. Before even making my way inside, they told me to go pack a bag and stay with them as long as I wanted. These are friends. They didn't go around gossiping and laughing. I could tell they truly felt bad.

There were also several people who went out on a limb to help me, even stepping out of their comfort zone, including Lieutenant Tim Williams of the Mishawaka Police Department and Marc Hardy, the longtime professor at Notre Dame who've both been mentioned. They stepped up and spoke on my behalf, explaining that one bad night was way out of character. They've remained good friends of mine.

Then there's a woman I met at work when we were in our twenties. Our friendship has been all over the place, but I know we can count on each other when it comes to real-life pain and heartache. Neither would hesitate to pick up the phone, regardless of how the last conversation may have ended. She was on a job interview nearly two years after the South Bend incident. Someone had mentioned my name because they knew she knew me. The person kept saying that I got a DUI in South Bend. She said, "Logan definitely did not get a DUI. For some reason, the cop asked her to take the Breathalyzer in front of her ex-boyfriend's house. So maybe that's why you think that? However, Logan was never driving and never stepped foot near a car." The woman was trying to argue with her, but she set the record straight. Most so-called friends wouldn't step up, especially in the middle of a job interview.

Keep Your Circle Small

I used to love the fact that I had dozens and dozens of friends. With age and experience, I'm proud to say I have five people who are REALLY my friends. I'm talking people who would go way out of their way for me and who know I would do that for them. They could care less if I were on television. I have a number of great friends/acquaintances as well who I enjoy hanging with on the regular. I'm not sure I would tell them my darkest secrets, but I like being around them. Life is hard. It's complicated, and it's scary. Not everyone needs to know your business to be your "friend."

My friend, Dali, wanted to add a little something on the example I mentioned about our friendship:

> Erin and I reacquainted at our high school friend's wedding. As most of our friends got married and had children, those friendships drifted. Erin and I, both being single, career focused and ambitious women, automatically gravitated to each other. Our paths were very common. On the outside we were masked individuals appearing perfect and unflawed. On the inside, we both were prisoners of our own demons and destructive thought patterns. We both did the "talk therapy" with not much luck. When we drifted apart, we coincidentally did group therapy around the same time. I think the perception that we had of each

other was probably similar. I looked at Erin as being beautiful, fashionable and a nice physique, as I struggled with mine do to emotional eating from trauma. I couldn't understand why she couldn't throw on something casual and just head out the door. It was as if the news industry she was in defined this perfect creature. As if she couldn't leave the house without looking like a 10. I just wished she could see herself as I saw her. I realize we can't see ourselves as beautiful and how others see us because when we looked in the mirror, we didn't feel worthy. She grew up with the perfect parents! I grew up with a single mother who gave me the world, but didn't know how to demonstrate affection or love. I couldn't deal with it and took a low blow at Erin. It wasn't right as she was going through a difficult time, which was why I invited her to come down and visit. I'm glad our friendship circled back and we picked up where we left off. We continue to work at our own personal growth grow every day and will not settle just to feel we have to "fit in" as the woman who married young and had a few kids.

CHAPTER 10

LETTING GO AND LIVING LIFE

"It's liberating to finally say that no other person is in charge of my happiness. I am. If somebody doesn't think I'm pretty enough, smart enough, or good enough, then so be it." As I read through this book, this line I wrote in chapter 7 made me smile again. We ALL know it to be true that only YOU can make yourself happy. Think about the guy who told you twenty times a day how beautiful you are or the boss who praised your work performance all the time. It probably made you feel good for an hour or a day, but if you don't think it or feel it, then what is the point? On the flip side, if a potential romantic partner is all set with you or a boss doesn't value you, then why torment yourself, ruin your day/week/month or more, and literally HAND OVER your power? Don't make the many mistakes I did in both situations. This is your life to live. Be you. Be authentic. Be confident. Don't change your hair, clothes, or makeup to impress others. People who matter accept you for you if you're a good, honest, caring person.

"One has to have compassion for oneself in order to not self-destruct. The mind is our constant companion. We have to make peace with it, control it, or it will crush you." These were my dad's words at the end of chapter 1. My mind was my biggest enemy. I didn't control it. It was telling me, "You're still the fat kid. You're always going to be someone's second choice. No one will like you or think anything of you if you're not on TV. Everyone looks at me differently because of South Bend, and they've created their own version of what happened as reality." Those days are over. I am NOT the fat kid. I will NOT be second choice or ever put myself in a position to be someone's second choice. If someone likes or doesn't like me because of a job title, then they are not worthy of my time or attention. As long as I know I'm worthy, that's all that matters. As for South Bend, I don't care what story people wanted to concoct and believe. The past is the past. I have no idea what the future holds; but with insight into what kept going wrong for me, forgiving myself and others, I'm pretty damn sure it's going to be a whole lot brighter than the picture the nasty voices in my head were casting for years and years. I will continue to work on creating the happy, well-rounded life I deserve. I will stop looking for *distractions* (my dad's least favorite word for good reason), and I will continue to make time daily to calm the mind.

Until the next book, I leave you with these quotes that I keep in my phone and glance at often when I feel an urge to entertain those negative, nasty, vicious voices.

> Love yourself. Forgive yourself. Be true to yourself. How you treat yourself sets the standard for how others will treat you. (Steve Maraboli)

> Release the past, let it wash away. Take back your own power. Stop dwelling on what you don't want. Use your mind to create what you "do want." Let yourself flow with the tide of life. (Unknown)

> When you settle for less than what you deserve, you get less than what you settled for. (Unknown)

> I've learned that if someone threatens my peace of mind, self-respect, or self-worth… I must walk away. I owe it to myself… I owe it to my future. (Steve Maraboli)

ABOUT THE AUTHOR

For nearly two decades, Erin Logan has been a familiar face in many local news markets across the country and most recently as an anchor in Cleveland and a reporter in New York City. Her passion for the business began in high school and grew deeper in college at Syracuse University and in graduate school at Boston University. Throughout her journalism career, she's learned a lot about herself and so many others. The common denominator—there are way too many of us who are not living in the present, putting an enormous amount of pressure on ourselves, and looking to others for "approval" as a measure of our self-worth.

In Erin's case, she allowed her job title to define her and could never fully answer her dad's question: "Are you truly HAPPY in ALL aspects of your life?" Once fully realizing the significance of that question, Erin has been a strong advocate for women and teen girls struggling with self-esteem issues. She created a program called REVIVE, a free series of workshops. She also got an online certificate in nonprofit executive leadership at the University of Notre Dame.

CPSIA information can be obtained
at www.ICGtesting.com
Printed in the USA
BVHW020304190422
634654BV00004B/46